With fresh biblical ins[ights] and gifted teaching, my li[fe and] church relationally thr[ough...chal]lenge the reader to foc[us...]

Dr. Dale Galloway
Pastor Emeritus – New Hope Community Church
Past Dean of Beeson Leadership Center at Asbury Seminary
Author and Speaker

Floyd's new book, *Follow the Leader*, is an insightful and practical work, a great new tool for the local church. Years ago, as a pastor wanting so badly to learn how to do small groups right, I went to a conference at New Hope in Portland. Since that time I have used everything Floyd has published on small groups. He really gets it and this latest work underscores that.

I am now a Natural Church Development/Church Health consultant. One of the eight essential elements of a healthy church is "Holistic Small Groups". Church leaders often tell me, "We tried small groups and they don't work here." Well, in every case, they were a far cry from being holistic and they certainly were not using the Jesus model Floyd describes in this book.

I contend it is virtually impossible to have a vibrant, growing church where people become wholly devoted followers of Jesus without a strong small group ministry that is done the Jesus way.

Ron Greeno
Transitional Interim Pastor Services
New Church Specialties

This is a must read for anyone who is serious about growing the local church – the only organization Jesus set up. *Follow the Leader* is looking back in order to look forward. Floyd knows what he is talking about. He gets what we so often miss . . . life change happens best in small groups. Buy one for everyone you know who participates in small groups. It will be money well invested as we seek to be the church Jesus had in mind, a relational one.

John Bishop, Senior Pastor
Living Hope Church, Vancouver, WA
Founder of the ONLY GOD network

I have invested the major part of my adult life researching, practicing and writing the very principles contained in Floyd's new book. He has captured the core of "doing the Gospel" while gathered in faith-based small groups. While reading *Follow the Leader* I have been reminded that the simple way Jesus did it is still the best way to be His people. This is the new handbook I recommend to those who want to do what Jesus did!

THOM CORRIGAN, AUTHOR AND SPEAKER/TRAINER
"EXPERIENCING COMMUNITY", "THE SMALL GROUP FITNESS KIT"

Follow the Leader is a fountain of refreshing spiritual insights to help you fulfill your personal call to make disciples. Floyd's years of experience takes this book from theory to where life is really lived—in relational small groups. You will discover "Follow the Leader" is also a practical guide as you take the next steps to become a leader committed to fulfilling the Great Commission. I highly recommend this "must read" book.

LARRY KREIDER, AUTHOR
INTERNATIONAL DIRECTOR, DCFI

Pastor Steve —
Blessings to you with
Hebrews 10:24 + 25

FOLLOW THE LEADER

FOLLOW
the
LEADER

Jesus with a Small Group

Floyd L. Schwanz

VMI PUBLISHERS • SISTERS, OREGON

Follow the Leader
© 2008 by Floyd L. Schwanz
All rights reserved

Published 2008

Published by
VMI Publishers
Sisters, Oregon
www.vmipublishers.com

ISBN: 1933204745
ISBN 13: 9781933204741

Library of Congress Control Number: 2008939687

All Scripture quotations are taken from the *Holy Bible, New International Version.* Copyright 1973, 1978. 1984 by International Bible Society. Used by permission of Zondervan Publishing House. All rights reserved.

Printed in the USA

Contents and/or cover may not be reproduced in part or in whole without the expressed written consent of the Publisher.

Cover design by Joe Bailen

Dedication

To all those faithful leaders who have said,
"Yes, Lord, I will follow You by leading a small group
entrusted to my care."
Each of you has honored me by letting me be your pastor/coach.
You gave me great joy when I saw the fruit of your ministry.
Your ministry will outlive your own life.
I dedicate this book to all of you because you helped inspire it.

Table of Contents

Foreword 11
Preface 13
Introduction 17
    The Church Is about Relationships 17
    Small Groups in Church History 18
    Doing Life Together 20
    My Personal Journey 21
    The Challenge 22

CHAPTER ONE: MARK AND HIS GOSPEL 25
    Jesus and the Twelve 26
    The Jesus Model 30
    The Jesus Strategy 33

CHAPTER TWO: CALLING THEM TO RELATIONSHIP 39
    Come to Me 41
    Follow Me 44
    Sharing a Life Together 47

CHAPTER THREE: WITNESSING THE MIRACLES 51
    Learning to Meet Needs 52
    Two Stories 53
    A Power beyond Themselves 54
    More than Hearing 56

CHAPTER FOUR: FACING OPPOSITION 61
    Breaking with Traditions 62
    Hurtful Words 66
    Hurtful Actions 69

CHAPTER FIVE: SOLVING INNER CONFLICTS 73
    Discovering Self Identity 74
    Competing for Position 76
    Learning to Trust 78

CHAPTER SIX: RECEIVING DEEPER TEACHING 83
    Away from the Crowd 85
    The Power of Dialogue 88
    Application Is the Destination 91
    Putting Love Into Action 92

CHAPTER SEVEN: LEARNING THE TEACHING STYLE 99
    The Contrast with Other Teachers 101
    The Inductive Method 103
    The Reproducible Method 104

CHAPTER EIGHT: SENDING THEM OUT 109
    Clear and Simple Instructions 112
    Accountability Is Essential 114
    Obvious Results Are Promised 117
    Four Words 118

CONCLUSION 121

EPILOGUE 127

APPENDICES
    A – The One-to-Another Mandates 129
    B – The Benefits of a Discussion Guide 133
    C – Principles for Effective Discussion Guides 135
    D – Redemptive Intimacy 137
    E – The Comparison of Discipleship and Evangelism 139

NOTES 141

Foreword

We have known for a long time that churches rise and fall on available leadership. One of the reasons we have experienced church attendance at an all-time low is due to the lack of lay leadership. Unless a church has a clear plan to develop church attendees into church leaders, the ebb and flow will continue downward.

The principles Jesus used in training His disciples apply directly to leadership training today. Jesus recruited a ragtag group of apprentices and transformed them into highly motivated leaders. The objective of Christ's ministry among the crowds was to convert them into disciples who would make disciples. Christ's purpose was always to prepare committed followers rather than enthusiasts. How did He do this? Through a relational small group process that continued on into the early centuries of the Christian history.

In *"Follow the Leader,"* you will discover how Christ prepared His disciples through reproducible small group methods. Floyd Schwanz guides the reader on a journey through the gospel of Mark to discover how Christ concentrated on the twelve rather than the multitude. You will learn how Christ's disciples were formed and prepared by participating with Him in His ministry. Floyd clearly articulates why a small group was the Jesus way to disciple a believer until they were able to also produce leaders rather than just large group attendees.

You will also catch Floyd's passion for the topic on every page. He lives what he communicates in this book. He is not just a theorist. He practices what he teaches. Floyd was a key staff pastor in the New Hope Community Church small group model in Portland, Oregon, with Pastor Dale Galloway. Later he became the small group pastor at the Wenatchee Free Methodist Church and the number of small groups grew to over 100 under his leadership. When I visited Wenatchee FM in 2003, I was super impressed by the quality of their small group ministry.

The principles to be discovered in this book are both biblical and practical. For many years Floyd has meditated on them, applied them, taught them and perfected them. His first book, *Growing Small Groups,* was a huge help to my own small group understanding in the mid-90s. I am certain you will find his newest book to be filled with the same profound insights.

JOEL COMISKEY, PHD
THE JOEL COMISKEY GROUP
INTERNATIONAL AUTHOR AND CONFERENCE SPEAKER

Preface

By using Mark's gospel as our text we will see the primary earthly ministry of our Lord was with His small group. He taught the crowds, but He trained the twelve. Only because of what He had done with them, were they able to do what He gave them to do in Matthew 28:19: "Therefore go and make disciples of all nations, baptizing them in the name of the Father and of the Son and of the Holy Spirit," and Mark 16:15: "He said to them, 'Go into all the world and preach the good news to all creation.'"

When Jesus said to "go and make disciples," they knew exactly what He meant. He wanted them to go out and do what He had done with them. TRAINING believers is more than just telling them. It is more relational than dispensing information to a large group by a speaker who is virtually unknown to the audience. It takes time, close up time—the kind Jesus gave the twelve. It includes knowing truth and learning how to apply it in daily life. Accountability in a climate of love produces the kind of fruit that a large group cannot produce. RAISING up disciple-makers is the outflow of this system. Just as parents raise their children and send them out, so a small group leader's success is realized when each member is successful away from the group to reproduce the ministry they have received.

This living illustration of a small group in action was made clear one summer when I photocopied the chapters of Mark's gospel in the center of each page. I then circled all the references to the disciples, such as: their names and words like: them, us, they, two, twelve, et cetera. When I saw the scribbles and brackets and arrows in the wide margins on each page, it became an overwhelming conviction to me that the vital ministry of Jesus with His small group has been almost overlooked. We have given unbalanced attention to what He did with the crowds and therefore our primary energy has been given to what we do with the crowds! Jesus followed an apprentice model and I am afraid we have settled too often for an academic one.

Question: Are small group ministries overlooked in the modern church?

Answer #1: Yes. Just listen to the conversation among church leaders, both clergy and lay! We have accepted a crowd mentality. Buildings and budgets, programs and events dominate our time and drive us to do more buildings and budgets, more programs and events.

Answer #2: Yes. Look at all of our activities. While our busyness looks like a prospering shopping mall, the souls of our people become shriveled for lack of nourishment.

Answer #3: Yes. We have filled our churches with consumers instead of producers. But let's not blame them. We have trained them to watch and listen and evaluate the program, hoping they will "buy in."

Answer #4: Yes. We have a serious lack of conversion growth, partly because I believe we have an expectancy that the clergy will "bring them in." We have said COME instead of GO.

Jesus emptied Himself of His heavenly culture in order to take upon Himself our human culture. He did not escape from His culture, but rather immersed Himself in it. Today we celebrate the incarnation and we follow His ways when we go into our world so His Kingdom will come on earth as it is in heaven. Like Jesus, we maintain the high standards of Scripture while we go into our earthly culture to make a difference. The gospel of our Lord Jesus is never diluted or substituted, for it goes wherever God's people go. Wherever we work, wherever we do business, wherever we recreate, wherever we go to school, wherever we live, the gospel goes.

If you have not noticed lately, not too many people are lining up to get into our churches. We must take up the model for ministry that our Lord gave us and take the Good News where the people are. Once they can get acquainted with Christ and His Word in relationships with Christ-followers, they will want to come to His church with us. In fact, I believe this is what the Apostle Paul had in mind when he said he wanted to "become all things to all men" (1 Corinthians 9:22). This is referring to getting into another person's culture, not about changing the gospel.

Many years ago I gave some time to consider what Jesus was saying after His resurrection in the John 20:21 assignment, "As the Father has sent me, I am sending you." How was He sent?

- He knew his Father's will.
- He was filled with the Holy Spirit.
- He did his primary ministry in and with a small group.
- His secondary ministry was with the large group.
- He expected opposition. He was not surprised by it.
- He fully expected results.

How are we to be sent?

- To know our Heavenly Father's will.
- To be filled with the Holy Spirit.
- To do our primary ministry in and with a small group.
- To do our secondary ministry with a large group.
- To expect opposition and not be surprised by it.
- To fully expect results.

Let's *Follow the Leader!*

Introduction

THE CHURCH IS ABOUT RELATIONSHIPS

Let's open our Bibles for a quick look at "picture definitions" of the church of Jesus Christ. Jesus said in John 15 that we are to be branches connected to the vine and that there is no life in us without that connection. But it is also apparent that we are also connected to each other in a web of relationships. 1 Corinthians 12 describes the church as a body with many and a variety of members, each one different and each one necessary for the body to function well. Together we are the visible body of Christ to a watching world. We are defined in Paul's first letter to Timothy as being members of a household of faith, brothers and sisters in the family of God. Peter's description is a picture of living stones being fit together into a spiritual house.

All of these are highly relational. The church of Jesus Christ is never referred to as a crowd/audience of people who do not really know each other. Obviously a church being a building is not found. Instead of God dwelling in a temple, we have become the temple where God dwells.

This reminds me of a pastor who was in a conversation with a friend and told him that his church was soon to celebrate their 100-year anniversary. His friend was surprised and said, "Oh, pastor, I have been by your church and it doesn't look that old!" To which the pastor smiled and said, "I don't pastor the building, I pastor the congregation that meets there."

The New Testament teaches us that our life in Christ is a corporate life. It is more than being together in one place while sitting in rows feeling friendly, but looking at the backs of people's heads. Also, I am sure you have noticed how few spiritual gifts are used in a large group gathering. God has given each of us special abilities to do some things well and life is so fulfilling when we get to use them, regularly meeting the needs of others as God has gifted us. We have opportunities often (not just occasionally) when we intentionally meet together to "stir up the gifts" and "spur each other toward good works." Instead of always watching others use their gifts, we all get to participate in a variety of ministries that multiply God's grace.

SMALL GROUPS IN CHURCH HISTORY

Moving forward from the first century to the eighteenth, we rediscover the relational part of being God's people in John Wesley's "class meetings." As the Methodist societies became a movement, Wesley instructed his preachers to "preach in as many places as you can. Start as many classes as you can. Do not preach without starting new classes." Even when the Wesley brothers were students at Oxford, it was their desire to develop a church pattern like the primitive church demonstrated…so different than the church life they were experiencing.

After visiting the major Wesley sites in England and reading extensively about his methods, I have come to realize their simplicity. They were not Bible study groups or the caring/sharing groups that we might expect. They were lay led and met weekly to give a report to each other about their lives, their activities, their temptations, their successes and failures as Christ-followers. It was received by all who participated as being a family experience because of their shared commitment to each other. They consistently encouraged each other to live life God's way and to do good things for the people around them.

The built-in accountability that helped those groups stay healthy was not a heavy-duty discipline for the people who were growing up in their new-found faith. It was there to help them become transformed into the image of Jesus! For many years I have regularly played the game of racquetball. As much as I love the game, there have been many times when I roll out of bed before dawn without any good feelings about having to go to the court and throw my body into the intensity of the game. But I go because I have promised a friend that I would meet him there! He is counting on me and I don't want to let him down. When we have given it our best, our shirts are wringing wet and we feel so good—so good. What a wonderful way to start the day. But it would not have happened without being willing to be accountable. I am convinced we all behave better when we know someone is counting on us.

A small group has a shared objective—to be Christ's followers in the daily routines of life. Back to the Wesley "class meetings"—many of those who attended were not yet what we would classify as believers. They were "awakened seekers" who wanted more than a weekly predictable religious ritual in a large group gathering.

George Whitefield was a fellow-member of Wesley's Holy Club at Oxford and became a powerful preacher. Near the end of his life, he sadly confessed that Wesley had fruit that remained that he did not have from his own ministry. He said it was because Wesley joined those souls who were awakened into small groups.

While in England to study Wesley, my wife and I had the opportunity to visit the National Museum of Coal Mining near Leeds. While waiting for our group to be called for the underground tour, we got to see various exhibits in the museum about the industry as it used to be. We were looking at various aspects of life in the coal-miner villages when my eyes saw the word "Methodist" in the framed explanation by the display. I grabbed a piece of paper and copied what it said.

> The early 19th century mining areas were wild and lawless places. But Methodism came to dominate the lives of mining communities. Drunkeness and swearing were not tolerated. The church also became a natural focus for their grief.

I realized again the value of small relational groups that Wesley called class meetings. Yes, they needed the open-field preaching by itinerant circuit riders to be awakened to God's love and what was offered to them through Christ. But, please notice the life-change not only happened individually, but also in community until entire communities (and a nation) were transformed.

It might be easy for us to think their lives were not as cluttered as ours and thereby excuse ourselves from being relationally involved with a small group of Christ-followers. When given the "too busy" reason, I am reminded of another quote from John Wesley in his eighteenth century that still speaks to us today in ours: "Make every class meeting an exhilarating feast of divine love and holy joy and people will come no matter how tired and/or busy they are. Fire is kindled with fire and wind. Enthusiasm is kindled with enthusiasm and the Holy Spirit."

I have had the privilege twice of visiting the Yoido Full Gospel Church in Seoul, South Korea, where Pastor Cho has also discovered the New Testament pattern. His people have shown the world how to grow very, very large by loving and growing people to be strong in their faith by forming cell groups all over that great city. Jesus was the first one to show us the apprentice system. Jesus showed us that we cannot disciple people in a crowd by only telling them what they need to know. We need to train them in a relationship, like a loving parent with the children God has entrusted to their care. Let's follow the Leader! And leaders like John Wesley and Pastor Cho.

DOING LIFE TOGETHER

Life change happens best where life is lived. Simple, is it not? A small group is where we get to "do life together." It is where we get to regularly take steps away from the "Jesus and me" mentality to the first century "Jesus and we" way of life. Away from our Me-thinking culture to a We-thinking one. Away from "It's all about me" to "It's all about we."

The "we" may only be two who are together, but Jesus is present (Matthew 18:19–20). Years ago a pastor friend told me about a Sunday when he was teaching his congregation about God's people being the church instead of the church being a building. As he was greeting people after the service, he was overjoyed to overhear two ladies making arrangements to have coffee together that next week. Their closing remark was, "I'll see you in church on Tuesday." He knew they understood the truth of his message that day!

MY PERSONAL JOURNEY

I did not begin my pastoral ministry with this concept in my heart and mind. I was taught biblical theology and church management, but was at a loss about how to disciple anyone. Part of that was because I was not discipled. I just grew up in a church program of services and classes and more services and classes. So I started out doing everything I could creatively do to have as many people as possible to attend the services and classes at our church. My version of what Jesus said would have been, "Where two or three hundred are gathered in Jesus' name, He is there." Therefore, most of my efforts were to get people to COME and try to make the large group event so exciting they would come back.

Through the years my concept of "church" began to change; slowly I became a "We-Christian." I have always been a highly relational person (as my family and friends would agree), but somehow I did not connect the way I was "wired" into my participation in church life. Looking back, however, I do not think I would have survived my early years in the pastorate without two factors: a group of four pastors who met regularly for care, prayer and learning from each other as well as a pastor in a neighboring city I could call on any time for encouraging support.

Sometimes in all of our lives we are overwhelmed, overcommitted and tempted to quit. It is not because the work is so hard or because our success is not easily measured. It is because we feel isolated and under-appreciated, under-supported. That is when we start trying to find a reason to resign that will help us take the step away and save face. Big things began happening in small ways a few years later when I was full-time in youth ministry with responsibility for more than three hundred junior and senior high school students. For the first time in my life I was forced to give ministry away. To the degree I was able to invest into the lives of my adult leaders, they were then able to disciple their small groups. This was quite a stretching experience for me, but I immediately saw God's hand in it. We still had the big events, but the training of Christ-followers happened best in small groups where they were more than just a name.

After ten years at Portland's New Hope Community Church, I moved away to a staff position in another city. After about a month, a lady stopped my wife and me after Sunday morning services to welcome us to the community and to the church. She asked if it had been difficult for us to move to a smaller church. When I answered that I hadn't even thought of that, she was surprised and said, "Oh, I know New Hope has thousands in attendance and we only have about 600." I said that was true, but I hadn't compared the two churches that way. As my wife and I drove home that day, I told my wife that what I told the lady earlier at the church was true. That is when I realized the New Hope way of "doing church" had changed me. Because we had more people involved in small groups than we had attending Sunday services, I no longer saw "church" as the Sunday gathering. I saw it as a family reunion of small groups! The church is wherever God's people are...scattered all over the community...two or more in His name.

THE CHALLENGE

Great sermons, the presence of God strongly acknowledged in worship and Bible classes that are power-packed are three things we need and want. But something's missing that the Bible says is vital: relationships with other Christ-followers. That is the life-to-life and heart-to-heart relationships that are more than acquaintances. Those kinds of encounters are where we get below the surface stuff and do the James 5:16 challenge to confess our faults to each other, pray for each other and then rejoice together in the healing.

To consider small groups to be some kind of a sociological fad would be to miss a primary part of Jesus' earthly ministry and what the apostles taught in their lives and writings. Jesus was not an office recluse who managed an organization. He was with the people—loving, forgiving, healing, instructing, training, giving hope and courage. His primary attention was to his primary group—the twelve apprentices. Their relationship with Him was like a laboratory. Let's follow the Leader by making each gathering of our small group a living-learning laboratory. We just cannot neglect the opportunity for the Christian growth that a small relational group provides.

DISCUSSION QUESTIONS

1. Of the New Testament picture definitions of "church," which one is most helpful for you and why?

    a. Vine and branches (John 15)

    b. Members in a body (1 Corinthians 12)

    c. Household of faith (1 Timothy 3)

    d. Living stones in a spiritual house (1 Peter 2)

2. From your own faith journey, how can you identify with George Whitefield's summary of his ministry and that of his friend, John Wesley?

3. Describe the advantages of both large and small groups and how neither is a substitute for the other.

4. Tell your group a story about "a journey marker" when you experienced a difficult time and God gave you someone to come alongside you.

5. What would the disciples have missed if they had only taken notes of what Jesus taught them, even if they had scored an A+ on the final exam?

Chapter One

MARK AND HIS GOSPEL

The gospel of Mark is a gospel of action. His writing style is simple and exciting—much like a child would tell the story of Jesus. Thirty-four verses are connected with "and" and "immediately" is used thirty times. Instead of just recording a historical event, Mark reports as if it was happening right before his eyes. He uses the present tense to emphasize the action he describes. Like the other gospel writers, Mark wanted his reader's lives to be affected in the present when he told them what happened in the past. It was like he wanted Jesus to be a contemporary person in all times.

Mark is the earliest of the four gospels to be written. It is the nearest record to being the biography of Jesus. Of the 616 verses in this gospel, Matthew reproduces 606 of them. Only twenty-four verses in Mark do not occur somewhere in Matthew or Luke. Mark's mother opened her home to groups of believers. Therefore, Mark was brought up with Christian fellowship as central to all he learned. His faith was formed in a community of the faithful.

Mark establishes the fact that Jesus Christ truly was the Son of God and that He was God incarnate. Mark establishes the fact that Jesus Christ was very much human, that His passions were like ours. Each gospel writer tells the life and ministry of our Lord according to what influenced them to leave all to follow Him. Even though we learn so much by studying these first-person stories, we also realize that not everything has been reported.

While reading Mark's gospel we are challenged to walk with Jesus. We visualize a scene or hear a word and somehow it speaks to the circumstances of our own lives today. He wants us to experience the Son of God, "The beginning of the gospel about Jesus Christ, the Son of God" (1:1) and be deeply touched by His message and method. Throughout the ages, those of us who respond to the call from Jesus have the promise and assurance that He will never abandon us, never reject us. He wants to be the One who leads us today even as He did with the twelve in those three brief years.

JESUS AND THE TWELVE

Mark also seems to be very careful to give us clear pictures of the twelve, both their triumphs and their failures. Sometimes very flattering and sometimes unflattering. He makes sure we understand that they had trouble getting a grip on the fact of His incarnation. His statement to them in Mark 10:45 was pivotal. He "did not come to be served, but to serve, and to give His life as a ransom for many." In so many ways we, too, are brought to think God's thoughts rather than our own. "When Jesus turned and looked at his disciples, he rebuked Peter. "Get behind me, Satan!" he said. "You do not have in mind the things of God, but the things of men" (8:33). Through their slowness to understand (and to sometimes misunderstand) He continued to prepare them for His absence. We have the assurance today that He will prepare us, too, as we endeavor to serve him by preparing those He has entrusted to our care.

There was quite some time between the time Jesus began teaching the large groups and His choosing of the twelve. It seems the time could have been as late as one year before the crucifixion.

> Jesus went up on a mountainside and called to him those he wanted, and they came to him. He appointed twelve—designating them apostles—that they might be with him and that he might send

them out to preach and to have authority to drive out demons. These are the twelve he appointed: Simon (to whom he gave the name Peter); James son of Zebedee and his brother John (to them he gave the name Boanerges), which means Sons of Thunder; Andrew, Philip, Bartholomew, Matthew, Thomas, James son of Alphaeus, Thaddaeus, Simon the Zealot and Judas Iscariot, who betrayed him. (Mark 3:13–19)

It is very apparent that their selection was far more than providing Him with traveling companions and observers.

He wanted to be sure they had learned to be, to do, to believe, to teach. They were to serve as apprentices, as interns, as students, as fellow laborers, as agents with the gospel. When Jesus gave the call to follow Him and become "fishers of men," He stated His purpose to have with Him those who would go to make disciples of others. Not only from His work, but also His actions help us understand the significance of His training of these men. In John 17:6 He prayed to His Heavenly Father that He had equipped these men as if it was the most important thing He had come to do. Except for being the Lamb of God, I believe it was. Except for announcing the good news that there is salvation through Christ, the most important thing God wants of us is to train disciple-makers. Let's follow the Leader.

Training a group of twelve was His plan; it was His only plan. Even though they were small in size, they were large in vision and assignment. Can God birth a movement in our day with the same simple design and power Jesus modeled with the twelve that was later seen demonstrated in Acts? Yes, in fact, cell-based ministries are exploding in many world areas! I pray it will happen where I am. Jesus was able to multiply himself through His small group. Because the gospel has come to us proves the success of His strategy! Jesus established the principle of discipleship in Matthew 10:24–25, "A student is not above his teacher, nor a servant above his master. It is enough for the student to be like his teacher, and the servant like his master. If the head of the house has been called Beelzebub, how much more the members of his household!" The apprentice disciple was to become like their master. Same message, same methods, same compassion, same servanthood, same suffering to be endured.[1]

The Apostle Paul moves us to an even higher goal where we are to be conformed to the image of Christ. "For those God foreknew he also predestined to be conformed to the likeness of his Son, that he might be the firstborn among many brothers" (Romans 8:29). The lesson here for us (as small group leaders) is that we are not better than other people because we are following our leader. We are all in need of salvation and then we become transformed by our association with Jesus the Christ and each other.

It has always fascinated me to look carefully at the group Jesus selected. They were men who had already shown a degree of sincerity in being around him. But they were ignorant of His intentions when He first called them, filled with Jewish prejudices and misconceptions. We find them to be slow to learn new things and to unlearn old things. Perhaps this is to help us find ourselves in God's call on our lives today. They had little or no celebrity status to flaunt. And here comes Jesus to call and train them to apostleship! I am encouraged to know that even today, whenever God finds a noble soul that is fully yielded, there is a measureless capacity for growth. What does God want to do with YOUR yielded life?

And have you ever wondered why Jesus chose twelve? He could have easily recruited more…or less. Perhaps our best reason for the significance of the number twelve is at least hinted in Matthew 19:28, "Jesus said to them, 'I tell you the truth, at the renewal of all things, when the Son of Man sits on his glorious throne, you who have followed me will also sit on twelve thrones, judging the twelve tribes of Israel.'" Could it be Jesus wanted to connect or bridge what He was doing to the twelve tribes all gathered under the royal reign of King David? If so, I know it would have fueled their desire that their participation would somehow restore Israel's political integrity and independence.

To be sure, the call the twelve received would be tested. They would be sharing in the popularity Jesus received, but also sharing in the pressure and hardship imposed by the religious leaders. Breaking with man-made traditions always has a price to be paid. Jesus told the stories of the new patch on an old garment and new wine in an old container to illustrate how the new and old do not agree. The twelve were being called to a radical new way…the way of the Nazarene. Throughout church history we see the price reformers have had to pay, but how thankful we are for their courage to stand with the Truth that went against the accepted traditions of their day. It would have been much easier to bow to "what had been" than to provide a new wineskin for the new wine of the Holy Spirit. When the disciples answered the call of the Master, they committed to unmatched adventure in a cutting edge ministry. We will also experience an adventure in spiritual growth when our hearts say "Yes" to His call.

Years later when the Apostle John looked back over his time with Jesus, he identified at least three marks of a true disciple:

He/she abides in His word (John 8:31-32)
He/she loves God's people (John 13:34).
He/she bears fruit (John 15:8)[2]

These things do not happen by just knowing the teachings of our Lord. As disciples we are called to obey what He has taught us.

> Therefore everyone who hears these words of mine and puts them into practice is like a wise man who built his house on the rock. The rain came down, the streams rose, and the winds blew and beat against that house; yet it did not fall, because it had its foundation on the rock. But everyone who hears these words of mine and does not put them into practice is like a foolish man who built his house on sand. The rain came down, the streams rose, and the winds blew and beat against that house, and it fell with a great crash. (Matthew 7:24–27)

Furthermore, He commissioned us:

> Therefore go and make disciples of all nations, baptizing them in the name of the Father and of the Son and of the Holy Spirit, and teaching them to obey everything I have commanded you. (Matthew 28:19–20)

Only then can the truth make a difference in our lives. If we are going to be like Jesus, we are going to need to do more then sing about it in church and listen to a lecture. The real life of a real disciple is in the real world, in the very midst of our culture's ways. Since we can no longer walk with Jesus physically on those dusty paths in Galilee and into Samaria and Jerusalem, we can still be His disciples and become disciple-makers. Let's follow the Leader! We have the advantage of having the Holy Spirit indwell us, to enable, to empower, to encourage us in every area of our lives.

When I first started living for the Lord in 1959, I knew **He** wanted to transform my life and that is what **I** wanted more than anything. But the whole concept was too overwhelming to me. I was counseled to live one day at a time, but the days for me were too long. So I started dividing each day into three natural parts: morning, afternoon and evening. When I woke in the morning, I asked Jesus to be the Lord of my morning and all morning long I trusted Him to guide me. When morning was gone I thanked Him for it and gave Him the afternoon. When evening came, I thanked Him for the afternoon and gave Him the rest of my day. It quickly became a habit that I still find myself following...almost fifty years later.

THE JESUS MODEL

I truly believe the earthly steps of our Lord were ordered in eternity. Not for one minute did He waver from His Father's will, from His objective. That is why we need to take a fresh look at how He did His ministry. Nothing was haphazard. No hurried spirit. No panic. He could not afford to take a chance because He knew His time was limited. This is so amazing when we factor the human element into the equation.

Without selecting a verse or two, here and there, let's look at the underlying pattern of it all. It is not a hidden pattern, but most of the headlines we have become familiar with are of Jesus teaching the crowds or serving the needs of people one-to-one. The pattern of His ministry is not hidden in the gospels, but it is so different than what we have become accustomed to follow in modern church life.

> *"Dear Lord, forgive us for offering our people only a rather impersonal program of services and classes and more services and classes. Help us to train and release our people to do ministry the way Jesus did—highly relational in our impersonal culture."*

Obviously I was not present, but I have been told that near the final days of Jesus' earthly ministry—after He had referred to the fact He was going to be leaving soon—one of the religious leaders came up to Him after the session and asked what would happen to His ministry after He was gone away. Jesus motioned toward the twelve who were standing close by and said He was leaving it all in their hands. His questioner looked over at the small group and then looked back at Jesus with a quizzical look on his face and asked, "What is Plan B?" The truth is: Jesus did not have another plan! According to John 17:4, it seems He felt very good about having completed the assignment His father had given Him. Really? With all of our emphasis on academia, I am afraid we would hesitate to trust these men with the commission of Matthew 28:18–20. But let's follow the Leader like they did!

WE CARE BEST IN A SMALL GROUP. Learning to care for each other was one of the biggest lessons the twelve had to accept. Jesus chose a very unlikely collection of individuals. Sons of Thunder, a Zealot and a tax collector, Galileans who were considered nonreligious. He chose none from the educated temple groups. The law of Christ is the law of love; it is the theme of His messages: to love God and love others. Jesus wanted them to love each other, not just tolerate those who were different. To truly love them as Father God loves them. Could it be that it is still God's plan for us to meet in small groups with people from widely different backgrounds, listening, sharing, forgiving, praying, caring and understanding each other? These lessons just cannot be learned while sitting in the rows of a weekend crowd.

Through the years I have watched the New Testament Greek word, KOINONIA, happen repeatedly in all kinds of small groups. This word is most often translated correctly with the word "fellowship." And as soon as we hear/read that word we think about a social happening. Being socially connected is an important part of who God made us to be, but *koinonia* (koy-no-knee-ah) is not a social word. It is much deeper and richer than that. It is a **spiritual** dimension that God wants us to experience. The literal meaning of koinonia is: the shared life, the giving and receiving of life, the exchanging of life. It is more than an acquaintance dimension where we get to know about a person. It is life at a deeper level where life is really lived.

Several places where the word is found include: Acts 2:42 where the Christ-followers devoted themselves to the koinonia; 1 Corinthians 1:9 where we are called into a koinonia with His Son and His Body of believers; 1 John 1:7 where we are called to walk in the light and when we do we will have koinonia with each other.

We train leaders best in a small group. Several years ago I was getting acquainted with a new small group of eight men. As we were briefly introducing ourselves, one man told about the congregation in a large city which had helped bring him to faith in Christ. They had nurtured him and he felt a great debt of gratitude to them. He had recently returned to his hometown and his home church and was shocked to find a dead church where forty years before there had been a very alive congregation. The founding pastor who had meant so much to him in his youth was no longer there and the church had now dwindled to just a few older adults trying to hold it together. The pastor had served all those years, but did not mentor anyone to take his place! As my friend finished his story he said, "Mentoring is what I call the bus concept." We turned to him with puzzled looks asking, "What's that?" He was quick to answer with something that continues to influence me—even helping to motivate me to write this book. His answer: "I want to live my life so if I should someday step off of a curb and be run over by a city bus, I can know that I have trained someone to take my place in the ministry God has given me!"

In the summer of 1997 I was influenced by Michael E. Gerber's book, *The E-Myth Revisited*. He skillfully explains why most small businesses fail when the entrepreneur only works to make the business succeed, instead of working to make the business attractive so someone else will buy it! He uses the McDonald's corporation to illustrate how they are not in the business of selling hamburgers—they want to sell franchises![3] To give away what they received is what Jesus wanted for the twelve. His primary work with them was with that in mind—a reproducible system. He called them, He trusted them, He taught them, He trained them, He loved them in such a way that they could go and do the same. The model He gave them was simple. It still is today! Are you up for the challenge of doing your ministry HIS way? Practical. Life-oriented. Relational. God-dependent. Let's follow the Leader!

While reading through Acts and the Epistles, we know how quickly they exercised His ways. When 3000 were added to the church on the Day of Pentecost, there were 120 who were ready to raise them up—making disciples out of believers. Those early churches may have been small in size, but they were certainly large in the way they viewed their work. His power unleashed in the hearts of fully devoted followers will make the difference today wherever you and I do our ministry. That is, it is if we will follow the Leader and allow the power of God to explode out of the upper room into the marketplace through meaningful relationships.

This book is about fulfilling the assignment of Matthew 28:19 by using the model Jesus gave us. Raise up believers in a small group until they are ready to go out and do the same with others. Our definition of disciple needs to be clear. There is no way we can know for sure if a person is a Christian because the Lamb's Book of Life is not opened to us. But I submit that we can know if a Christian is a disciple. How? If they are living for Jesus by grace and by choice, being with Him in order to become capable of doing what He does and becoming what He is. That is the basic definition of the word.[4]

THE JESUS STRATEGY

The small group of twelve had a lifelong history of Passover and other similar festivals and activities. Jesus now comes with a new way to measure life…LOVE (See John 13:1–35 and 1 John 3:14). Wow. Is that the bottom line? Loving God and loving each other? Loving God through awe-inspiring worship (individual and corporate) and loving each other through healthy small groups. What would happen if we dropped all the programs we have created in the last fifty years and put the same effort into obeying the Great Commandment and the Great Commission?

Could it be that the humility, the simplicity, the realness, the serving as evidenced among the twelve would still be a powerful force today? Could it be that high-touch ministry is what our high-tech culture needs?

Jesus' strategy was a risky one. So was the plan Jethro gave to his son-in-law, Moses, in Exodus 18:17–27. Can you imagine the fear Moses must have experienced as he gave the "untrained" leaders of ten the responsibility of making decisions about real needs? It was probably similar to the risk we take when we give away formerly clergy-driven ministry to "untrained" but redeemed and Spirit-filled people of God!

> *"Lord Jesus, help us to discover (or re-discover) the joy and wonder and deep satisfaction of Your life-giving plan."*

While giving myself to an intense study of Mark's gospel I suddenly realized how often the twelve were mentioned and the motivation for this book was born.

As I went back through my pages of scribbles, I was able to categorize some key areas of insight that have become the chapters for our consideration. The list of forty-one is by no means an exhaustive one, only enough to help us give our attention to the Jesus way of doing ministry with a small group.

Calling Them to Relationship

    Mark 1:16–20
    Mark 2:15–17
    Mark 3:31–35
    Mark 6:31
    Mark 14:17–21, 26

Witnessing the Miracles

    Mark 1:21–34
    Mark 4:35–41

Mark 5:1+
Mark 5:25+
Mark 5:37–43
Mark 6:35–44
Mark 6:47–52
Mark 8:1–9
Mark 11:20–21

Facing the Opposition

Mark 2:15–17
Mark 2:18–22
Mark 2:23–3:6
Mark 7:1–23

Solving Inner Conflicts

Mark 9:33–37
Mark 10:1–27
Mark 10:32–45
Mark 14:29–31
Mark 16:14

Receiving Deeper Teaching

Mark 4:10+
Mark 4:33–34
Mark 7:17–23
Mark 8:14–21
Mark 9:28–32
Mark 10:10–12
Mark 10:23–31
Mark 10:32–34
Mark 13:1–4+
Mark 14:22–25

Learning the Teaching Style
> Mark 8:27–30
> Mark 13:3

Sending Them Out
> Mark 3:13–15
> Mark 6:7–13
> Mark 6:30–32
> Mark 16:15–18
> Mark 16:19–20

DISCUSSION QUESTIONS

1. Agree/Disagree. By giving so much time to the twelve, Jesus showed He was not concerned for the needs of the multitudes. Please explain.

2. What could be a reason why Mark reminds us repeatedly that the twelve did not fully understand the message or the ministry of their Leader?

3. Paul and Barnabus were only in Thessalonica for five months. How could a church (as described in 1 Thessalonians 1:1–10) come out of such a brief ministry?

4. What can be done to encourage the spiritual growth of Christ-followers today?

5. In our culture, how can we best raise up and train disciple-makers?

Chapter Two

CALLING THEM TO RELATIONSHIP

History is clear: the most sweeping and significant revivals began as small group movements. John Wesley's legacy for example, reveals the genius of his organization and the desire to raise up a holy people in healthy small groups.

It was shocking to me to discover recently a quote from Fidel Castro which confirms Jesus' discipleship strategy: "I began my revolution with 82 men. If I had to do it again, I would do it with 10 to 15 men and absolute faith. It does not matter how small you are, providing you have faith and a plan of action." We know that the focused action of a few dedicated people can change the course of human history, while the undisciplined actions of a crowd achieve little. The Jesus group of twelve has multiplied through the centuries as small groups continue to meet and minister in His name around the world today!

In the ministry of Jesus, knowledge was gained by association before it was fully understood by explanation. Before He sent the disciples out, He wanted them to be with Him.[1] For Jesus to spend His primary energy and time with the twelve seems at first glance to be a mismanagement of what He came to do, namely "to seek out and save the lost." It seems that when He did get down to His "short list," He most certainly could have found those who would be better qualified. We would probably be tempted to recruit the extrovert who meets people easily and can always find a way to engage in a conversation. Or we would want someone with a better-than-average understanding of biblical truths, and also someone with some teaching skills to accompany their Bible knowledge. And, of course, we would want someone with some years of experience in an effective prayer life.

While rereading what I have just written, one of my favorite stories comes to mind—a real-life illustration. A small group leader I had the privilege of coaching was converted at age fifty-five. He was a career cab driver in Portland, Oregon. After he came to place his faith in Christ, he always had his Bible next to him in the taxi because it opened many conversations about spiritual matters. Harold loved to share what God had given him: freedom from sin, purpose for living and heaven as his destination. His cab company only charged half-fare for cancer patients, and a new ministry opened for him. He loved talking with customers who needed transportation to and from doctor appointments and therapy treatments.

It was not long before I received a call from Harold to ask if I would assist him at a funeral. The family of a man he had helped come to faith in Christ had asked Harold to do the graveside service. He stopped by my office to take me to the cemetery on the appointed day. About twenty-five people were gathered, and as soon as the funeral director was ready to begin, Harold thanked everyone for coming, led in a brief prayer, related how he met his friend and how he had trusted Jesus to be his Savior and Lord. He opened his Bible to read some scripture (I think it was a psalm) and made some very appropriate comments about how God was with his friend during the months of his suffering and how God was with us now. He closed with prayer and turned it back to the funeral director.

I was so blessed just to be there! He wanted me to assist him and I did. I went with him and stood there. On that afternoon that is all he needed as he led his first funeral and had never been to "funeral school"! When I got back to my office, I realized how he learned to minister like that—so personal, so relational and with the Word of God. It happened every Thursday evening when he and his dear wife welcomed a small group into their home—a little rough around the edges, but used of God in a mighty life-changing way. Harold was not someone we would have probably chosen out of a crowd of Christ-followers to be a small group leader. He certainly did not have the typical "leader qualities," but God's good news was too good for him to keep. His response was to be an instrument of a changed life to help life change to happen in someone else's life. He was not educated and skilled as a speaker/leader, but, oh, how he could relate with the joy of God's grace.

Before second guessing the way our Lord recruited His small group by deciding how we would have tried it, let's look again at His recruiting method.

COME TO ME

"Come" is the first of Jesus' words we see in Mark 1:16–20 that we can also use when we gather our small group together. Come is a simple invitation that even a child can understand. It is also direct, not cluttered with the need of further explanation. (i.e.: "Just as I Am, I Come") Come is also personal and individual. So relational, in fact, that the invitation can be received as person-to-person even while being in a crowd. One more important part of "Come" is how it leaves people with the freedom to choose: To come or to stay where they are, to change or to stay as they are. To hesitate is to refuse the invitation. To come—for them and for us—means to change direction, leaving the former, more familiar and safe ways. For those we invite to visit our small group we simply describe where and when and what and then say, "Come."

"Come to me" has such an endearing tone to it. It is an invitation we find repeated many times in the life and ministry of our Lord.

To weary disciples in Mark 6:31: "Because so many people were coming and going that they did not even have a chance to eat, he said to them, "Come with me by yourselves to a quiet place and get some rest."

To the children in Mark 10:14: "When Jesus saw this, he was indignant. He said to them, "Let the little children come to me, and do not hinder them, for the Kingdom of God belongs to such as these."

To the heavy burdened in Matthew 11:28: "Come to me, all you who are weary and burdened, and I will give you rest."

To a full surrender in Mark 10:21: "Jesus looked at him and loved him. "One thing you lack," he said. "Go, sell everything you have and give to the poor, and you will have treasure in heaven. Then come, follow me."

To Lazarus in John 11:43: "When he had said this, Jesus called in a loud voice, "Lazarus, come out!"

To the hungry disciples in John 21:12: "Jesus said to them, "Come and have breakfast." None of the disciples dared ask him, "Who are you?" They knew it was the Lord."

Please notice with me that His recruiting invitation was not to a creed or to a certain prescribed curriculum or even to a length of time. It was relational. It was come to ME! "'Come, follow me,' Jesus said, 'and I will make you fishers of men.'" (Mark 1:17)

Jesus was the Son of God—fully human so He had relational needs just like we do. The twelve needed Him, but He also needed them. He taught them in real-life experiences as they moved around the various regions. He wanted them to have a real-life legacy when He was gone – more than the completion of a course of study. We can follow His methods, no matter the culture where we serve.

He was to be the center of their newly formed community. He saw them as potential leaders, but He was **the** leader. We know so little about the twelve before Christ called them. The faithful writers of the gospels did not bother to research all the minute details of their past lives. That must be because Jesus was to be the theme, not them. They needed this time with Him, to see how He related to His Abba Father, to see how He depended totally on the power of the Holy Spirit in order to go and help others in multiplying small groups to know Jesus, His Father and the Holy Spirit.

Jesus broke through many barriers in the religious culture of His day when He selected the twelve. His entire ministry demonstrated the fact that fishermen, zealots, tax collectors, publicans, Samaritan women, could all have fellowship with God.

To accept the fact of their relative obscurity we must also acknowledge the huge witness their lives have since made in the world. Jesus did not want (or even see the need) for more than one Peter-type in His small group. Each one of the twelve had his unique and absolutely necessary gifts and interests. Those of us who are of the more common sort are sometimes able to do some things even better than some of our more celebrated brothers and sisters!

It would be a mistake to try to recruit our own small group of believers solely because of their common culture. If any common element can be identified other than Jesus, the group may get sidetracked into being an 'other-than-Jesus' group—perhaps well-intentioned, but side-tracked nonetheless.

God wants our unity to be from the oneness we have in the Holy Spirit. Homogeneous groups of believers were hard to find in the first century. They were heterogeneous: Jew and Gentile, slave and free, men and women. God by His Spirit wants us to be formed into one body that has diversity in our unity. Please realize the unity Paul explains in his epistles is not having agreement in ideas and opinions. Never! It was because of primary relationships within the church. Not in the church building because they did not have those. It was unity when they were gathered **as** the church. Filled by the Holy Spirit, they formed a powerful fellowship.

A funny little smile comes to our faces when we see the twelve together—a tax-collector with a tax-hater, the one who worked for the hated government with the one who prayed for Rome to be overthrown. Could it be that this was God's design to help us understand even today that every small group is to be a church in miniature, a germinating church? If this is close to being true, then we should not close our doors to the "grace-builders" who visit our groups. Jesus wanted His small group (and ours) to know that to be devoted to Him means we love and accept people who are not like us.

There is no question about the motive and purpose of Jesus' choosing the twelve. They were in a very non-accepting culture and He wanted to change all that. The religious leaders avoided the publicans and sinners. The Jews were repulsed by the Samaritans. Non-Jews were regarded as pagan. Women were the servants of men. Children were considered property. Jesus placed high value on every person, regardless of gender, race, age or social status. And He invited them to His group!

There must be great wisdom in Jesus' deciding to pour His life's energy into such an assortment: fishermen, revenue agents, political malcontents. After He left His ministry in their hands they were no longer known as fishermen, revenue agents and political malcontents. They were known as those "who had been with Jesus" as we see in Acts 4:13: "When they saw the courage of Peter and John and realized that they were unschooled, ordinary men, they were astonished and they took note that these men had been with Jesus!" Governmental persecution and lack of formal education did not seem to be a hindrance to them. The most significant revolution in human history began as a Jesus-led small group. Vitality is always mightier than size!

In my own mind I have come to the conclusion that Jesus chose the twelve because they were ready and fully willing to be discipled. He was not overlooking the educated, the wealthy, the CEO's of his culture. He chose the twelve because they were willing to submit to being a disciple of the Nazarene from a carpenter's home.

FOLLOW ME

The twelve were called to be with Jesus as He continued His ministry and mission. It is also our mission to give our groups the authenticity of being "in Christ." Notice again what happens in Mark 1:16–20:

> As Jesus walked beside the Sea of Galilee, he saw Simon and his brother Andrew casting a net into the lake, for they were fishermen. "Come, follow me," Jesus said, "and I will make you fishers of men." At once they left their nets and followed him. When he had gone a little farther, he saw James son of Zebedee and his brother John in a boat, preparing their nets. Without delay he called them, and they left their father Zebedee in the boat with the hired men and followed him.

Immediately after Simon and Andrew were called to be fishers of men, they accompanied Jesus to watch and participate in the recruiting of James and John. They quickly understood that a call to follow Jesus was a call to do ministry with Him. They had responded to the challenge of being productive "fishers of men," and before very long at all they saw it happening!

The "follow me" invitation which was given to Matthew in Mark 2:13–17 is with a different context.

> Once again Jesus went out beside the lake. A large crowd came to him, and he began to teach them. As he walked along, he saw Levi son of Alphaeus sitting at the tax collector's booth. "Follow me," Jesus told him, and Levi got up and followed him. While Jesus was having dinner at Levi's house, many tax collectors and "sinners" were eating with him and his disciples, for there were many who followed him. When the teachers of the law who were Pharisees saw him eating with the "sinners" and tax collectors, they asked his disciples: "Why does he eat with tax collectors and 'sinners'?" On hearing this, Jesus said to them, "It is not the healthy who need a doctor, but the sick. I have not come to call the righteous, but sinners."

Levi (his old name) was collecting government fees at Capernaum where Jesus was very much at home. He would have had many opportunities to see Jesus before and for Jesus to have seen Levi. But on that day the timing was perfect. The call to follow was not a cold call and, therefore, his following would not be a blind leap of faith either. He had seen and/or heard of lepers being cleansed, demons being cast out, blind receiving sight, Jairus's daughter being raised. The most noteworthy part of the account in Mark is in 2:14 when he responded unhesitatingly—not to a program, but to Jesus. And also to a life with the other disciples!

When our sins are forgiven after we have confessed our need of Christ and turned from our sinning to fully trust Him, we are saved. But, beloved, we are saved into a family. Even Romans 10:9–10 (If you confess with your mouth, "Jesus is Lord," and believe in your heart that God raised him from the dead, you will be saved. For it is with your heart that you believe and are justified, and it is with your mouth that you confess and are saved) was written to a Christian community where confessions were heard and public baptisms occurred.[2]

Our culture has put such a high value on individualism that we often refer to Jesus as my "Personal Savior." To allow ourselves to buy into a "Jesus and Me" mentality is to ignore a major part of the New Testament. It is "Jesus and WE." To attend a weekend worship service and "accept Christ" is a good start. To be connected with a group of brothers and sisters in Christ is vital, rightly related to God and each other as we journey together.

The call we all respond to is to Jesus **and** to those He has given us in our "household of faith." It is a double commitment for us. First John 3:16 reminds us that God loves us and that we are to love each other in the same way.

In the beginning days, the twelve were believers in Jesus as the Christ, the Promised One. They had personally witnessed several events (John 2, 3, 4): the wedding, a Passover, John's ministry, the Samaritan woman's conversion. As they left their secular callings to this higher calling they did it with deep resolve and purpose. Jesus refers to this again in his prayer recorded in John 17:6. The only way His ministry would continue was if they were able to receive some on-the-job training from Him. His ministry had to be founded on the solid rock conviction of a few, not the shifting sand loyalties of the crowds.

The twelve were recruited from a much larger number of disciples to receive special training. This helps us understand that "following Jesus" was more than physically being with Him that the twelve enjoyed. A disciple is one who has counted the cost, made a commitment of faith and serves in His name. Once the response to His call was made, it became the beginning of a brand new life and the putting away of the former life. Even though the crowds followed Jesus in a physical way, they did not follow Him with life-changing commitment. And God still calls people to step out of the crowd and follow as a disciple. He still calls the curious to personal obedience to His way, putting full faith in Him as Savior and Lord.

SHARING A LIFE TOGETHER

There is something almost sacred about eating together, about singing together, about praying together, about being afraid together, about doing ministry together. Jesus provided this kind of a "family" learning environment for the twelve. But, please notice they were not exclusive.

In all their sharing of a life together, they also shared life beyond themselves (Mark 9:35–44). Jesus and the twelve worked together to give life to all. Jesus wanted to model for them a separated life, yet a life lived out among others in the community. It is Jesus and the three (Peter, James, John), Jesus and the twelve, Jesus with the seventy, Jesus with the one hundred and twenty. In so many places it is Jesus and the twelve in the very midst of public ministry. It is Emmanuel (immanently with us) in the intimacy of a small group as well as Emmanuel (transcendently with us) in a large group.

Have you ever wondered why Jesus chose only twelve **men**? Why were there no women apprentices in this core group for training? Gareth Icenogle in his book, *Biblical Foundations for Small Group Ministry,* suggests that they needed a new understanding of their masculinity (pp 209–210). They needed a group experience with Jesus to be released from an unhealthy dependence on negative patriarchal modeling which dominated their culture. He wanted them to embrace a new model of how men could relate to God and to each other, to women and to children. He knew they needed to be radically transformed from their cultural perspective. He wanted them to be empowered by a new family system where they would be servant leaders.

The small group Jesus established became His family (Mark 3:31–35 and 10:29–31). In Matthew 18:18–20, God promises that when two or three of us gather with our brother, Jesus, we are able to access God as our father. Wow, what a family – an eternal family! Even though we are still on earth, we have a direct connection to heaven.

As with so many of our small groups, there may be one or more who make us wonder how they got in! This is certainly true with the Jesus "group." How did Judas get into such a holy fellowship? But note the direct words about this during the foot washing when Jesus said, "I know whom I have chosen." It helps us know that we may also choose those who will later dishonor the call to be with Jesus. If that happens, we know that Jesus knows what we are going through. It must have been so difficult for Him to carry the secret burden of knowing what was in Judas's heart.

What had Jesus ever done to Judas to cause him to betray his master? Basically, all He ever did was to see through him and expose him. Many times a close fellowship alone is enough to expose a sin-filled heart. Also, Judas knew that the opposition was becoming more intense. He wanted to be safe and he decided to save himself. The one who at one time had helped cast out devils (Mark 3:13–19) was now filled with the devil himself.

Now we need to look briefly at the life of the small group in their closing days. Mark 14:50 records that when Jesus was arrested late on that Thursday night, the small group ran to hide. "Then everyone deserted him and fled." They came back together after His death and resurrection to be with Him again as "family." Except now they began to understand how His initial call was to participate in an eternal life as well as the earthly one. God's desire is for us to have the shared life, the exchanging of life, the koinonia with Him and with each other FOREVER!

I trust you realize how much God wants us to live in "a community of believers" as we walk out of the audience of hundreds of weekend worshipers. If Jesus made the recruiting and training of a small group His high priority, can we do less? Small group leaders are raised up in healthy small groups, not from the church pew. Classroom training is informational, but not formational unless there is accountability. Relational leaders are formed in relational groups in the midst of real-life issues. Every time a small group meets, it is a laboratory with Jesus for spiritual growth and leadership development.

It is evident when we open our Bibles to the four gospels that Jesus had a leadership strategy. Not a crowd strategy or a numbers strategy. He did not play to the crowds, because He knew how fickle their loyalty could be. By His own model of raising up this small group to reproduce what He had done with them, the multitudes could be reached and cared for. Let's follow the Leader.

Calling Them to Relationship

If Jesus invested a lot in a few, then we need to invest a lot in a few. Therefore raising up new leaders is to be the long-term goal of small group ministry. If I would rewrite my first book, I know I would change very little. But I know I would change the title. Instead of *Growing Small Groups* it would be *Growing Small Group Leaders*. Having good materials and good methods won't float the boat. ==The key is having an increased number of growing leaders.== More than the development of technical skills, what we need is spiritual openness, a serving attitude, Spirit-led discernment and a deep passion to reach the unreached. The skills needed to lead a dynamic group can be learned along the way. The Jesus kind of small group is about relationships—with Him and with each other. Grow them up and send them out.

Review for yourself all the "one to another" mandates in the Epistles (Appendix A) and ask yourself how these are being obeyed in the lives of the people who worship together with you on a weekend? How will these things happen if we are only with each other in a shopping mall type church? Perhaps in our coming and going a few "one to anothers" will happen by accident. But if we view them as more than great suggestions, we will give opportunities for them to happen intentionally and regularly every week. Of course, I believe the best place to follow through with the one-to-anothers is in the ongoing life of a small group of Christ's followers. His disciples do these intentionally.

God wants more than to get us through to heaven. He wants to create us to be **a people** who share His life and character together, regularly, face-to-face, life-to-life and heart-to-heart. Jesus demonstrated this for us in His small group. Let's follow the Leader.

DISCUSSION QUESTIONS

1. What is your definition of the word DISCIPLE?

2. Why was it important to Jesus to have such diversity among the twelve He recruited?

3. What are some of the reasons a person might give who does not choose to participate in our small group?

4. If you were choosing a small group of people to train as disciple-makers, what would be some of the qualities you would look for in them?

5. What are some of the ways the call of Jesus to discipleship comes today?

Chapter Three

WITNESSING THE MIRACLES

Part of the apprentice system Jesus was demonstrating for us included having his small group watch and actually help with several miracles. By spoken word and simple action the normal course of nature was set aside, revealing God's power and presence to them. However, Jesus and the twelve did not just travel around from village to village to do tricks for people. They had no desire to just **show off** God's power. The miracles recorded in the gospels were to meet the real needs of people. The following list of nine references includes the need(s) met and the bigger lesson Jesus wanted them to learn. Their future ministry would need the conviction that came when they themselves had witnessed God's workings, not just hearing a report from someone who was believable.

REFERENCE	THE MIRACLE	NEED MET	BIGGER LESSON
Mark 1:29-34	Peter's mother-in-law	In bed with fever	Power and Authority
	Many Sick Many Possessed	Diseased Enslaved	Demons recognized Him and He wouldn't let them speak.
Mark 4:35-41	Winds & Waves	Boat almost swamped	Creation obeys the power of the spoken word. Fear or faith?
Mark 5:1	Demon possessed	Lived among tombs and cut himself	Set free and restored to right mind
Mark 5:25	Hemorrage	12 years bleeding and spent all	Faith exercised with only a touch

REFERENCE	THE MIRACLE	NEED MET	BIGGER LESSON
Mark 5:37–43	Daughter raised	12-year-old died	Witness a resurrection in preparation for his death. Death is only sleep.
Mark 6:35–44	5000+ are hungry	Are fed and satisfied in a desolate place	Little is much. The miracle was in their hands
Mark 6:47–52	Walked on water	Rowing against the wind and fear possessed.	Preparation for their future. "Take courage; don't be afraid"
Mark 8:1–9	4000+ are hungry	Nothing to eat for three days	Miracle again in their hands
Mark 11:20–21	Fig tree cursed	Non-bearing	Faith releases power (i.e. mountain into the sea)

It seems that an integral part of the ministry of Jesus (and subsequently His small group) was healing. In no way was it a side issue. We see Him going to teach and heal, repeatedly the two went together. The healing miracles were not incidental results of pity, but an expression of His conviction that He had come to redeem the whole person. Perhaps there may be a few who would prefer having Jesus as a small group leader who only socialized and taught a little lesson. To eliminate the supernatural from your thoughts of Jesus you would still have a wonderful leader. But you would not have the miracle-working Christ of the Bible.[1]

Living in a love relationship with God and others will help me see needs of the people around me and get them connected to the One who loves to meet them at the point of their need.

LEARNING TO MEET NEEDS

Jesus came preaching a gospel of love. He taught that He was sent from heaven because Father God so loved the world. He introduced us to the seeking love of God in stories like the three in Luke 15. After participating in a few miracles the twelve had the confidence to "just do it." They were sent to heal, to raise the dead, to cleanse lepers and to drive out demons. Imagine! And all this without a training program by our standards. They came back, however, with reports of success (Luke 10:17–24).

Did this ever open their eyes to the needs all around them! They now had visual testimony of how God wanted to touch the lives of people through their lives. They were taught how to trust God to meet the real needs of people, not to spend God's power only on themselves. Jesus never did a miracle only for Himself. The thrust of His life was to serve rather than to be served.

How do we follow the Leader in this chapter's theme? Answer: By welcoming prayer requests and praying "in the name of Jesus" for each need in our group as it is presented. Many times we have seen the miracle power of God unleashed as we gathered in our small group's "circle of faith" to trust God and God alone. Family members reconciled. Marriages healed. Unemployed employed. Oppression lifted. Barren to give birth. Sick raised up. Timid given courage to speak up. Houses sold. New ministries conceived. There's nothing to compare with being part of a miracle in someone's life! To be up close and personal when God comes on the scene in a miraculous way convinces everyone in the group that the God of miracles delivers.

Living in a love relationship with God and others will help me to better see the needs of the people around me and get them connected to the One who loves to meet them at the point of their need.

TWO STORIES

We are familiar with Paul's admonition in Galatians 6:2 to help carry each other's burdens. The people we have in our groups are ready to do that, but before the carrying can happen there must be some sharing. When there is a trust factor, when each person knows the group is a safe place, when they know what is said in the group stays in the group, then there will be sharing. For example, I was visiting a church in Montana when a couple came to me with a small group story about a miracle. Toward the end of their group's meeting they were embarrassed to admit that they had a medical need and not enough money to cover it. The group prayed and someone said they should put a bowl on the kitchen table if anyone wanted to help with some cash on their way out that evening. When the host's son came home later from work, he asked his mother what the cash was for in the bowl on the table. When she told him he opened his wallet and threw in a little more. His mom counted the money and called the couple to let them know the amount. To the dollar, it was the exact amount they needed! The son's last minute contribution had made the difference.

One of my favorite need-meeting stories comes from Wichita, Kansas. A single mom with two small children had just moved to town. She had visited a small group only twice, but knew they loved her. When she was absent that next Wednesday, they tried to call but got no answer. After their meeting one of the couples stopped by her house. She was home and said she did not have enough gas in her car to attend the group and also to get to work the next morning. When the phone rang that evening, she knew it was probably them. She did not want to answer it because she was embarrassed about her predicament.

In the conversation the couple found out she was behind on her rent and also her utility bill. Before the following Sunday, when I heard the story, that small group paid her rent and the group that had birthed their group paid her utility bill so her electricity would not be shut off. After the pastor finished the brief interview and the congregation cheered, he turned to them and asked a very good question, "If trouble comes to you this week, who are you going to call?" Here she was, alone in a big city and overwhelmed with problems beyond her control. Even though she was attending the church she would not call the church office because she did not know anyone there. She did not even call her small group—they called on her because they were related!

A POWER BEYOND THEMSELVES

The ability to do the supernatural was now made available to the Jesus small group. But as they went into their ministry, they were certainly mindful of the fact that they were extensions of His ministry. They were to go in His name and therefore He was expressing a huge trust in them. This means He was standing by to back them up no matter how fierce the opposition was that could be mounted against them if they were serving and proclaiming in His name. He never let them underestimate the power of the enemy, but constantly taught them to depend on Him (1 John 4:4 is ours today as well). "You, dear children, are from God and have overcome them, because the one who is in you is greater than the one who is in the world." They were sent as sheep among wolves (Matthew 10:16) and therefore they would need to be directly connected to the miracle-working God, not to their own strength and cleverness. "I am sending you out like sheep among wolves. Therefore be as shrewd as snakes and as innocent as doves."

Years ago my brother moved to do missionary work in Haiti and left me with a Power of Attorney to take care of his business while he was out of the states. With that piece of paper I was able to sell his house and even get into his safety deposit box at the bank for something his daughter needed. One day while praying "in Jesus' name," I suddenly realized that I was exercising an authority very similar to what my brother had given me. I dropped my head in deep humility when I realized how long I had had the power of Jesus' name and had not done much at all with it. I went home and found the properly signed paper and used its form to write the following:

> KNOW ALL MEN BY THESE PRESENTS, That I, the Lord Jesus Christ, have made, constituted and appointed and by these presents do make, constitute and appoint Floyd L. Schwanz my true; and lawful attorney, for me and in my name, place and stead and for my use and benefit, to use every spiritual gift and every opportunity, giving and granting unto my said attorney full power and authority to do and perform all and every act and thing whatsoever requisite and necessary to be done, as fully, to all intents and purposes, as I might or could do if personally present, hereby ratifying and confirming all that my said attorney shall lawfully do or cause to be done, by virtue hereof.
>
> Signed and dated by the Lord on the date of my conversion.

My prayer life since that time has never been the same. I learned to pray as a young child in a Christian home and to close my little prayer with the phrase "in Jesus' name. Amen." As an adult I still said those words, but without knowing the authority that was mine when I prayed in the name of the One who gave me the authority. I wonder what miracles are waiting to happen in our small groups? God waits for us to come to Him with the authority of Jesus' name?

It must have been a startling clarion call on the night before His crucifixion when the twelve heard Jesus say they would do greater things than He had done (John 14:12). Really? After all the miracles they had witnessed and now He is declaring in a matter-of-fact way that they would do more. More? Yes, and then He goes on to explain how the Holy Spirit would come and empower them. In His earthly ministry Jesus could only be in one place at one time. While He was ministering to the needs of a few, so many others needed him. While He was in a personal encounter with the people in one village, how many other villages needed Him? With the Holy Spirit's enabling, they could be seeing these same miracles all over the area at the same time.

Healing. Delivering. Calming. Dispelling Fear. Providing. Etc. Because of the miracles they had actually participated in, they knew now that nothing was impossible with God.

MORE THAN HEARING

Have you ever visited the Grand Canyon in Arizona or Bryce Canyon in Utah? If you have, then you have your own stories and probably your own photos. And have you tried to describe it to someone who has never visited those awe-inspiring places or has never even seen a photo? What do you say to someone who has never experienced the wondrous beauty of what has been sculpted in those two places? I have tried and have decided to just encourage them to make every effort to go see for themselves. My words alone are not enough.

How would you ever describe a sunset at the beach to a blind person who has never seen one? The power of seeing that brilliant sphere begin slipping down over the distant horizon? The vivid colors that stretch across the sky and at the same time a bright stream of gold extends across the water all the way to where you are standing on the beach? Mix the pageant of what I have just described with the gentle splashing and washing of the waves across the sand and words alone are not enough. I am so thankful I have experienced beautiful sunsets at various Oregon beaches many times. They are mine, even though I have trouble describing a sunset to someone who has never seen one at the beach before. They are beautiful, but you'll just have to take my word for it.

One of the undeniable miracles of God that the twelve experienced was to discover the warmth and love in their small group. I am sure when they first met and looked at each other it was quite a challenging dynamic as they "measured" each other. They quickly realized how much they were all in need of forgiveness. They knew they each had their own imperfections. True community is the only place that can heal us and free us so we don't have to keep our masks on. The walls come down and we don't have to keep pretending anymore that everything is okay when it is not.

We can love and be loved; we can listen and be heard; we can touch and be touched; we can give hope and encouragement and also receive the same. Not only did the twelve need Jesus, they also needed each other more than they realized when they first came together.

Isn't it sad that so many in our culture never "find themselves" in a caring group? It is because they look in the wrong places. Invite them to your group where the life of Christ is celebrated each time you come together.[2]

It is such good news that God can bring together a "mixed" combination of persons into a small group, and before very long they become healed and go to bring healing to others. I will never forget a report I received from a pastor friend about a small group in his church. He knew a lady in their group had been diagnosed with cancer and was not given a favorable prognosis. He knew the group would suffer a deep grief when she died. So he was not surprised to see them huddled together at the cemetery after the graveside service, crying and holding each other in love. He walked closer to offer help and that's when he realized her husband had just given each of them the notes his wife had written before her death. Little personal notes that said, "Thank you for loving me;" "Thank you for praying with me;" "Thank you for taking care of my family;" "Thank you for giving yourself to me." Their tears were grief-induced but also blended with thanksgiving that they had entered into each other's lives in such deeply meaningful ways.

I could also tell you how God has been at work in my family in so many miraculous ways, but those would only be my stories. You need your own. I could tell you about miracles of changed lives in churches where I have pastored, but those would only be my stories. You need your own. I could tell you what I have witnessed firsthand as I have seen God's power at work in several world areas, but you need your own stories. You need to know for yourself how God's miracle-working power makes a difference in our day and time. He still works through people like us.

It is amazing to see God work outside of the natural order of things. Mere words are so limited to be able to describe what we have experienced. The twelve found this to be true in Mark 6:47–52. They had just witnessed the feeding of the 15,000 to 18,000 people and yet when the storm came upon them they were terrified. Jesus helped them get ready for their future by reappearing in the midst of the storm. Instead of helping them, He frightened them even more. As soon as He was in their boat, the storm settled down and they were amazed (Mark 6:52). "They had not understood about the loaves; their hearts were hardened."

What does God want to do in showing Himself to be the Almighty as He meets the needs in your small group? There is no substitute for the way a real live miracle increases our faith and deepens convictions that we can trust God with anything. Let's follow the Leader and release God's power to meet the real needs of people we know and love.

DISCUSSION QUESTIONS

1. How did the authority Jesus exercised when doing the miracles also cause the people to hear what He had to say when He taught them? (Mark 1:27–28)

2. What are some of the ways the twelve got to participate in the miracle of Mark 6:30–44?

3. Where do you find yourself in the miracle story of Matthew 14:22–32?

   __ Watching from the shore?

   __ Watching from the boat?

   __ In the boat, but not watching?

   __ Nervously ready to step over the side?

   __ Hearing Jesus call you, but still seated?

   __ Walking toward Jesus?

   __ Going down and crying for help?

   __ Embraced by Jesus after you were down?

4. Do you believe Jesus wants us to continue his ministry of healing? If so, how can we best do that as a small group of believers?

5. Name one miracle that someone you know really needs. Is this something God can handle or is it too big for God? Please explain.

Chapter Four

FACING OPPOSITION

The small group became a safe harbor for the twelve as they continued to face increasing opposition and harassment from religious leaders. Jesus gave them a safe place where they could learn to respond in a healthy way and be healed at the same time. They learned to be free, yet holy. In this way they were able to continue doing what was right, even though they were severely criticized. They had a home base (their small group) where they could regroup.

Do our people need a safe place in our day as we face an anti-Christian culture that seems to be more and more hostile against Christian values? When taking a stand against some of the popularly practiced sins, we can expect opposing opinions and attitudes, perhaps even hurtful words and actions. We have the courage to keep standing firm when we know we are not alone. Solomon referred to this kind of reinforcement in Ecclesiastes 4:8–12.

> There was a man all alone;
>   he had neither son nor brother.
> There was no end to his toil,
> yet his eyes were not content with his wealth.
> "For whom am I toiling," he asked,"

and why am I depriving myself of enjoyment?"
This too is meaningless—
a miserable business!
Two are better than one,
because they have a good return for their work:
If one falls down,
his friend can help him up.
But pity the man who falls and has no one to help him up!
Also, if two lie down together, they will keep warm.
But how can one keep warm alone?
Though one may be overpowered,
two can defend themselves.
A cord of three strands is not quickly broken.

I found a quote from John Winthrop, Early American Puritan leader, that speaks directly to the distinguishing characteristic Jesus desired for His small group. In the same way these immigrants in 1630 faced hardship and opposition, so did the disciples Jesus was leading into "a new land." Winthrop's vision of community life was: "We must delight in each other, make other's conditions our own, rejoice together, mourn together, labor and suffer together, always having before our eyes our community as members of the same body."[1]

BREAKING WITH TRADITION

We need to do a close review of four places in Mark's gospel that illustrate how Jesus and the twelve faced opposition to help us with our own. The first is at the home of Matthew for the celebration of his decision to follow Jesus.

> While Jesus was having dinner at Levi's house, many tax collectors and "sinners" were eating with him and his disciples, for there were many who followed him. When the teachers of the law who were Pharisees saw him eating with the "sinners" and tax collectors,

they asked His disciples: "Why does he eat with tax collectors and 'sinners'?"

On hearing this, Jesus said to them, "It is not the healthy who need a doctor, but the sick. I have not come to call the righteous, but sinners." (Mark 2:15–17)

Matthew invited many of his friends from his "old life" so they could meet the One who had helped him be set free. Luke 5:29 says that the party was a great one. Jesus was the honored guest, accepting and enjoying the opportunity to be with Matthew's friends. Outside, however, the occasion was seen as scandalous. Pharisees from Capernaum and Jerusalem were putting the pressure on the disciples with their questions about why Jesus would do something so contrary to popular customs. Jesus stepped up to answer them Himself with grace and truth, "The physician needs to be with his patients."

Another lesson for life came as the religious leaders asked why the twelve were not fasting like the disciples of John.

Now John's disciples and the Pharisees were fasting. Some people came and asked Jesus, "How is it that John's disciples and the disciples of the Pharisees are fasting, but yours are not?" Jesus answered, "How can the guests of the bridegroom fast while he is with them? They cannot, so long as they have him with them. But the time will come when the bridegroom will be taken from them, and on that day they will fast. "No one sews a patch of unshrunk cloth on an old garment. If he does, the new piece will pull away from the old, making the tear worse. And no one pours new wine into old wineskins. If he does, the wine will burst the skins, and both the wine and the wineskins will be ruined. No, he pours new wine into new wineskins. (Mark 2:18–22)

Jesus again used this as a teaching opportunity to explain what was missing in their own lives. Fasting had become too mechanical, a matter of keeping another one of the many rules. Jesus said there needed to be a purpose for it, not just a time and place. He followed that by giving two parables: the new patch on an old garment and new wine in an old wine skin.

The disciples were again able to handle the pressure caused by their being "found guilty" of breaking with tradition because they had each other. Jesus made sure they had a safe place. Throughout church history, the Reformers like Luther and Wesley faced severe opposition when they led people away from long-standing church traditions. Those who eulogize the past say that the old wine is the best. It is mellow, mild, fragrant and whole bodied. The new wine is too harsh, too fiery. An old wineskin cannot contain it. We need to know our past so we can respect it and honor it. But we are not to worship it.

A better explanation of this by our Lord is found in Luke 5:36–39. He told them this parable:

> No one tears a patch from a new garment and sews it on an old one. If he does, he will have torn the new garment, and the patch from the new will not match the old. And no one pours new wine into old wineskins. If he does, the new wine will burst the skins, the wine will run out and the wineskins will be ruined. No, new wine must be poured into new wineskins. And no one after drinking old wine wants the new, for he says, "The old is better."

Mark 2:23–3:6 records another tradition breaking event that caused more trouble for Jesus and the twelve. They actually got caught plucking some grain heads as they walked through a field on the Sabbath. This was a religious "crime" and they were guilty. I think they knew what they were doing would cause trouble, but they must have been hungry. So they did it anyway.

This is one of six recorded instances when the Sabbath rules were broken. Five were when Jesus healed people on that day and this one because they were" working" (reaping and threshing). In each case Jesus referred the religious leaders back to God's original design. The Sabbath was made for mankind, for **our** benefit. The Sabbath was never intended to be a burden.

It was and is to be a gift from God so we would not rob ourselves. Jesus did not cancel it, only explained how they had taken the Sabbath in their own hands by writing so many rules and regulations about it.

The last illustration of the growing opposition for us to review is in Mark 7:1–23. The Pharisees were watching with fault-finding attitudes and saw the twelve eating with ceremonially unclean hands. The answer Jesus gave them was another "just in time" teaching opportunity. Jesus was not only answering for Himself, He was answering for their actions too. He came to their defense. He quotes Isaiah 29:13 to help their accusers realize that the real issue here was not about cleanliness. Jesus wanted them to know they could be very seriously ritualistic and be morally contaminated. He wanted them to look past the artificial duties they had imposed and were so anxious to enforce. He wanted them to examine their hearts, the control center from which their lives were really lived.

Of course I am only guessing, but it is my opinion that most of the twelve (if not all) would have succumbed to the pressures if they had to face them alone. Because they enjoyed the safety of the group, they were able to take a deep breath and go out to face the next one! They also had the chance to dialogue together with Jesus after each episode and a new understanding of Kingdom living was the result. Have there been times when a small group has provided a safe harbor for you? When you have been misunderstood? When you or someone you love has been treated unfairly? When the opposition comes from a source that you thought was your friend?

As we have seen in all four of these examples, the twelve were able to stay free at the same time they lived holy lives. They gained strength each time to bear up under opposition when their ways were considered unacceptable and different. A few years later, Peter and John stood with boldness before the Sanhedrin because they had become spiritually fit through their struggles against previous accusations. They could do what was right, no matter how they were criticized. Their example is an inspiration to us. Let's follow their example and provide "standing power" for each other.

Do you have some people in your small group who are members of

"The Barnabus Club?" Barney was an encourager. The Apostle Paul writes an invitation to the Thessalonians (1 Thessalonians 5:11) to encourage and build each other up—to join the Barnabus Club so to speak. When opposition is coming from inside or outside, we need the Barneys to speak up. Their words are life giving, affirming and generous with praise. They affirm people for whom they are, not for whom they wish they were. Even the most disagreeable, critical and unloving person has at least one good quality that a Barney can find. One more thing about Barneys that make them so special in the life of a small group: They know how to graciously accept expressions of appreciation and commendation when they are given to them.[2]

I wonder who the encourager was in the Jesus-led small group. Who are the ones in your group besides yourself?

Their small group was a training ground, a laboratory. What is God getting us ready to face? Together we stand; divided we fall. This is part of the great success the twelve-step program of Alcoholics Anonymous has enjoyed. Every person in the group knows, "We're in this together." I had a dear friend who invited me to go with him to his weekly AA meeting. What a joy and what rich insights I received. On the way home that night I found out that everyone has a sponsor and most everyone is a sponsor for someone else. He told me that was how he stayed sober. He had two people who were counting on him to stay in the program—one who had been sober longer than him and one who had recently gained his sobriety. He was not alone as he lived with the temptation every day to go back to the bottle. He had a small group and he stayed sober for himself **and** for them.

HURTFUL WORDS

One of the ways small groups will have opportunity to provide a healing for each other is when unjust accusations or even name-calling has come. Of all places in the community, the community of believers must be the place where hurts can be freely admitted and encouraging words received like a soothing salve to the wound. What are the words that speak **life** to you?

What are the words that speak **death** to you? "From the fruit of his mouth a man's stomach is filled; / with the harvest from his lips he is satisfied. / The tongue has the power of life and death, / and those who love it will eat its fruit" (Proverbs 18:20–21).

When meeting together and the group senses that someone has been hurt, we need to look inside ourselves and discern what we have received that can administer a healing touch to another person. I am not referring to some profound and eloquent words, nor to search for words with which we can dispense a wealth of information—as if we know so much on the topic. What needs to flow is the transcending power of the love that Jesus gives. Love heals.

When we have trouble seeing only the mess of a situation, we need to look a little deeper. We need to be reminded of Zephaniah 3:17 that the God of heaven sings over us! "The LORD your God is with you, he is mighty to save. He will take great delight in you, he will quiet you with his love he will rejoice over you with singing." This is the wonder of the gospel. We declare it to each other when we are living with the pain of hurtful words. I think it is sad that so few of the people we meet in worship on the weekend have experienced this dimension of spiritual community. With all the psychological studies that have been done in the last one hundred years, one thing is certain: When you are hurting, it sure helps to talk to someone you trust! And someone who will listen with the heart.

Recently my wife and I had the privilege of attending classes with Dr. Larry Crabb at Regent College in Vancouver, B.C. His word to us was to do three simple things whenever we wanted to provide a healing fellowship for another person.

1. Listen to the Holy Spirit on their behalf.
2. Spiritually read to see what the Holy Spirit might be stirring.
3. Enter into their dark night and together wait for the light.

His counsel was to constantly be reminded that the life we want to give to another person is in God's Son. "And this is the testimony: God has given us eternal life, and this life is in his Son. He who has the Son has life."

(1 John 5:11–12a) It is HIS life we are trying to stir up in the person who has been the victim of a verbal hit.

It is time to admit our churches are filled with broken people. People who want to turn their chairs toward each other because they know they cannot make it alone. They are then able to look beyond each other's wounds, worries and washouts to see what is alive and good.[3] Sitting in a crowd, it is so easy for us to make it appear how unbroken we are. But while sitting in the audience we long to be loved at our worst. To know we are not our problems. We are not the wounds. We are not our sins—as ugly as they might be. We are persons of unrevealed beauty.[4] I pray that each of God's people will find a place that is safe **with** a few people, not safe **from** people.

As the Jesus-led twelve began experiencing hostile attitudes, I am certain the conversations when they were together (though unrecorded) centered on their own feelings and what the future might hold for them. Considering their finding a safe place with Jesus even though surrounded with trouble, I am reminded of a Henri Nouwen quote in Larry Crabb's, *The Safest Place on Earth* (p. 37):

> We probably have wondered in our many lonesome moments if there is one corner in this competitive, demanding world where it is safe to be released, to expose ourselves to someone else, and to give unconditionally. It might be very small and hidden. But if this corner exists, it calls for a search through the complexities of our human relationships in order to find it.

I am sure you have felt the pain along with another person who has shared theirs with you. Because of your love for them, their hurt has somehow become yours. Then for those of us who share life with a small group, we will understand Galatians 4:19 with the Apostle Paul, "Dear children, I am in the pains of childbirth until Christ is formed in you!" We take on a parenting role and as much as possible provide a safety from the world who will oppose us from time to time. Again, Dr. Larry Crabb gave excellent help to us at this point. We are not to pretend we are trained therapists and feel that it is our responsibility to "fix" the problem. Instead, we help them discover God's power at work. We know the love of God that is administered with a human touch is better than advice anyway! It dries the tears that no one can see. It heals the hurts that cannot be expressed in words. If there is truth in the gospel of Jesus Christ, then we can never lose hope, no matter how serious the situation.

HURTFUL ACTIONS

Opposition really began to heat up when the small group approached the time of Jesus' arrest, His trial and death. Fear was overwhelming them in the garden of prayer and continued through the night and into Friday. They scattered like sheep. Jesus had just instructed them to not be troubled with their trouble. "If you believe in God, believe also in Me," he had told them. But instead, they put their faith in their feet and ran. They did not have faith that night that their Lord would return or faith that they would even survive the weekend.

Luke 22:31–32 gives the words of Jesus as He tried to prepare His small group for this crisis time. "Simon, Simon, Satan has asked to sift you as wheat. But I have prayed for you, Simon, that your faith may not fail. And when you have turned back, strengthen your brothers." He said it would be a sifting time when the chaff and the wheat are separated. They had a two-fold challenge: many followers had left and now their leader would also be gone. Jesus had tried to help them be able to receive spiritual benefits they could not have imagined would be theirs through this crisis. When they did meet Him face-to-face in His resurrected body, He told them to celebrate the victory and then to strengthen others. He wanted them to devote themselves anew to more labors of love. The crisis became a turning point in their spiritual journey. They knew how important it was now to provide a safe place for each other when the pressure was on and hurtful words and actions were being felt.

Small groups such as those designed to help with specific needs (substance abuse, compulsive behavior, parenting, marriage, divorce, grief) all provide a safe place for life issues to be confronted. But every group that has Christ in the center can help each other make commitments with high accountability to confront the hurts that have come from other people's mean-spirited words and actions. They know that their group will back them up with encouraging support, much like Jesus did with His twelve. Let's follow the Leader.

DISCUSSION QUESTIONS

1. After reading Mark 7:1–23, how is it that things that are originally designed to help people follow God end up being traditions that are somehow more important than following God?

2. How can we live with Christ's law of love in a culture that does not acknowledge it as relevant?

3. What could you say to a person about what it costs to follow Christ before he or she makes that decision?

4. What has been the cost you have paid because of your commitment to Christ?

5. Name three people you know who need to be encouraged because you know something about the trouble that has come to them. How will you express your thoughts to them this week?

Chapter Five

SOLVING INNER CONFLICTS

Every family has them. Every small group, every work place, every school, every athletic team, every church has interpersonal stresses and misunderstanding, differences of opinion and selfish ambitions, competitive words and actions that destroy the unity of the Spirit. It happened many times as the twelve lived, worked and traveled together. By meeting them at their points of conflict, Jesus helped them find themselves. They needed the give-and-take in group life so they could remain competitive without being hard on each other. Jesus helped them (and us) with some real life lessons of learning how to trust each other and grow up. He taught them that the way of the Kingdom of God is the way of serving. And, yes, that also includes the giving of ourselves to a cross.

It is very important for us to know the difference between a group and a class. Jesus and the twelve model for us the difference in this chapter. There is a teaching that happens in both, but classes are primarily content-oriented, whereas groups are life-oriented. It is not mere telling our group the accurate and needed information. Jesus let them raise the issues and then gave the underlying principles for them to then apply. This kind of personal need-meeting ministry happens best in a small group because that is where real needs get exposed.

We will see the small group leader, Jesus, rebuke occasionally, but always with compassion and genuine humility. He is the God of the second chance. We will see Him often answer their probing questions by asking them a question. Why would He do it that way when He certainly had the answer? Because He wanted them to discover truth on their own. Only then would they be equipped to succeed when He was absent. More than pat answers to pesky questions, He wanted them to interact with Him and each other. As a result, the level of their learning would increase. And that is group life at its best!

DISCOVERING SELF IDENTITY

Jesus and the twelve were traveling from the Mount of Transfiguration toward Capernaum. Jesus was thinking about the coming betrayal, the suffering and the cross. The twelve were thinking about their rank and position in the Kingdom. Since Peter, James and John had been selected to a higher privilege they thought they also deserved something special above the others. Upon reaching Capernaum, Jesus began teaching them about humility and showing preference to those around them. He knew if they continued quarreling among themselves, their effectiveness in ministry would be severely hindered. His days were numbered and their selfish, prideful wills needed to be addressed.

When Jesus asked them what they had been arguing about, they had nothing to say.

> When he was in the house, he asked them, "What were you arguing about on the road?" But they kept quiet because on the way they had argued about who was the greatest. Sitting down, Jesus called the Twelve and said, "If anyone wants to be first, he must be the very last, and the servant of all." He took a little child and had him stand among them. Taking him in his arms, he said to them, "Whoever welcomes one of these little children in my name welcomes me; and whoever welcomes me does not welcome me but the one who sent me." (Mark 9:33–37)

I have been in that spot, haven't you? When I know I have had the wrong attitude and have no excuse, it is better to just be silent! They must have also realized that He already knew what had been said. The little WWJD bracelets are a constant reminder that the Lord is present and all words and actions are known to Him.

In order to be as forceful as possible while making His point, He did not yell at them. Instead, He brought a child into His arms and talked about being childlike! A child is a child without intending to be one and now Jesus is challenging the twelve to choose to deliberately be lowly in their hearts instead of being so ambitious. He was not asking them to depreciate themselves, but to do the work of the Kingdom with a submissive spirit. Of course, His was the perfect example as He sat before them as the Son of God and yet humbling Himself to be the least. Jesus continued His teaching by calling on them to receive the child as they would receive Him. They were to give no thought of serving the weak and helpless as being too far "below them." It was important for Jesus to move into this area because He knew if their primary thoughts in the future were about their ambitions, then their actions would also rank others. As a result, some would be deserving of their attention and others would not.

Jesus concludes this teachable moment by warning them not to serve those who could give something back, but to seek out and serve those who could not give much of anything in return.

How can we follow the Leader as we watch Him with the twelve? We can avoid filling all the spaces in our time together with our own agenda of what we want to talk about. Jesus let those who were entrusted to His care to raise the issue, either by word or action. We, too, can seize the teachable moments that God gives us and depend on the Spirit's help to make them count with redemptive responses. This is one of the major differences between a class and a group. Interruptions are welcome in a group.

In many of our churches we still have the mistaken idea that we make disciples in a classroom with a thirteen week course of study. We can give lots of helpful information in a few weeks, but to disciple a person in the ways of our Lord means "to train" him/her with accountability takes time. Instead of trying to read their minds, we scratch where they itch. They will tell us. Those in Jesus' small group told Him. Let's follow the Leader.

In Matthew 19:3–12 Jesus is able to do a further teaching about self-sacrificing actions. The contest is the questioning by the Pharisees about marriage and divorce, "Is it lawful for a man to put away his wife for any and every cause?" Jesus' answer was filled with sympathy when He said it would be better for a man not to marry in the first place. By answering this way He was not judging one better than the other, but honored both. Then Jesus began explaining how important it was to renounce material things, not just family relationships. The bigger lesson here that they needed was to value self-sacrificing actions. This sparked Peter to ask what they could expect since they had done so much for the Kingdom of God. To this Jesus assured them that they would indeed be rewarded, but being faithful should be their highest ambition. Serving is a higher calling than being served.

COMPETING FOR POSITION

On their way to Jerusalem for the last time together (one week before the crucifixion) Jesus had just announced for the third time that suffering was to come (Mark 10:35–45). The twelve were dreaming of thrones since He had just been discussing Kingdom principles with them. They seemed to be almost giddy as they envisioned their places of privilege.

James and John coveted the highest **positions.** These are the same two disciples who resented the rudeness of the Samaritan villagers.

> As the time approached for him to be taken up to heaven, Jesus resolutely set out for Jerusalem. And he sent messengers on ahead, who went into a Samaritan village to get things ready for him; but the people there did not welcome him, because he was heading for Jerusalem. When the disciples James and John saw this, they asked, "Lord, do you want us to call fire down from heaven to destroy them?" But Jesus turned and rebuked them, and they went to another village. (Luke 9:51–56)

Now they were elbowing their way into a superior place above the others in their small group. They also had the assistance of their mother with less than sincere humility! Their request really upset the others in the circle who were certainly upset.

I am not sure the two brothers had given much thought to the effect their request would have on the other ten, but selfish driven people seldom do. Before we scandalize their zeal, let's not be afraid to look at ourselves. They were foolish and offensive, but so are we. When we have been presumptuous and irreverent, we need to ask Jesus to help us with **our** selfish ambition, pushing our way for our own purposes. I am sure we each have our own examples of what happens when favor is given to flatterers instead of those who are more "spiritually qualified" in our opinion.

In the narrative the twelve saw the widow being given commendation for what she had done and they wanted a promotion in the here-and-now. Twenty-four ears waited for Jesus to handle the inner conflict that James and John had caused. Unity had been broken in their small group, not unlike what happens in the life of our family/small group. What does Jesus do? He again tries to help them with the bigger picture rather than the immediate one.

Like a parent to a childish child Jesus spoke with a mild yet direct rebuke. He spoke to both the offenders and the offended, the two and the ten.[1] There was compassion and correction, but also instruction: the way to the throne is the via dolorosa! I think they answered too quickly when they blurted out that they were ready to travel the way of suffering. Jesus responded by saying, "Okay then, you will drink of my cup and you will be baptized with me." He made it sound like they were going to receive a favor, even though it would not be what they envisioned. He was teaching them about the heavenly kingdom that would be theirs when He gave His life as a ransom. With His pending suffering on his mind, He talks about the coming kingdom in contrast to the earthly one. He wanted them to know that the things as they were now were so different than they would be someday.

As "parents" of a small group, sometimes the best we can do for those who are entrusted to our care is to lift them up above the immediate concern to help them with perspective that the "helicopter ride" provides. In my own life (and when I have tried to help others with the bigger picture) I have turned to Paul's word to the Corinthian believers. My paraphrase of 2 Corinthians 4:16–18 is, "The things that are seen are temporary, are passing. The things that are unseen are eternal, are permanent." It is true, when bad news comes or when everything seems to be going in reverse or someone else gets the promotion or _____, we lose perspective. All we can see at the moment is the problem, the mess or the broken dream. The words from Jesus about the heavenly kingdom were His attempt to help His small group to look up to the eternal.

LEARNING TO TRUST

Jesus had been hinting several times that He was going away and an alarm bell went off in Peter's head.

> You will all fall away," Jesus told them, "for it is written: "I will strike the shepherd, and the sheep will be scattered. 'But after I have risen, I will go ahead of you into Galilee." Peter declared, "Even if all fall away, I will not." "I tell you the truth," Jesus answered, "today—yes, tonight—before the rooster crows twice you yourself will disown me three times." But Peter insisted emphatically, "Even if I have to die with you, I will never disown you." And all the others said the same" (Mark 14:27–31).

Peter was facing his own danger and uncertainty as well as the soon separation from his small group leader. When Jesus said some would fall away, Peter quickly said he would never forsake his Leader, even if all the others would. The way Jesus responded to his super self-confident statement was like He was talking to a child who was bragging on how tough he was. The problem was that Peter did not think of himself as a child. He wanted to be a man. Jesus simply wanted Peter to more honestly see himself and experience a form of spiritual crisis. Peter had faced self-revealing occasions before, but this one on the eve of the death of his Lord was deeper than the other episodes. He was told he would be a coward and would run away when the pressure came. This must have been like a dagger in Peter's self-confident heart. But it was the making of Peter in those hours!

I am sure if the reader has been active in a small group, you will have your own memories of a similar situation. Someone blurts out their own strong opinion about themselves and everyone looks to the leader to handle it. What did Jesus do? First of all, He avoided the put-downs or name-calling. Second, He knew Peter well enough to know He could be direct in what He said, perhaps more direct than to some of the others. In a sense Jesus was giving words of caution. "Not so fast, Peter. Give it some thought. These are perilous times for all of us. We will all be pressed to the limits, so much so that even you will not be able to stay with me like you would like."

Leaders lead with compassion at the same time they are honest about the issue at hand. Perhaps we could call this "The Velvet Hammer"!

After the glorious resurrection, Jesus appeared bodily for the fourth time (first to Mary, then Peter, Mr. and Mrs. Cleopas (in Luke 24:32), now the eleven). Jesus convinced them with the facts of who He was physically. (Mark 16:14). "Later Jesus appeared to the Eleven as they were eating; he rebuked them for their lack of faith and their stubborn refusal to believe those who had seen him after he had risen" (Mark 16:14), Then He explained how His resurrection was the fulfillment of Old Testament prophecies.

Did they gain a full understanding of Christian doctrine with this brief discourse that evening? No, but for the rest of their lives they would be students. This time with their Leader was like receiving a single ray of light into the shadowy places of their minds. The daylight of God's truth always penetrates the darkness! The eleven could probably echo the response of Mr. and Mrs. Cleopas, "Our hearts burned within us, too!" Receiving truth has the same effect on us in our small groups. Testings—such as they experienced the weekend before—have a way of drying the wood in our souls, making them ready to burn.

Until this time their selfish ambitions had made them slow to learn.

Now, on this evening, they were ready to hear with their spiritual ears.

Satan continues to scatter seeds of division in Christian communities. If those seeds are allowed to grow they will destroy the very koinonia we treasure. If you are active in a small group, face this enemy squarely. We will always suffer trouble when we compare ourselves with others, condemning and judging in order to justify our own position or opinion. Grace needs to be given and serving others is the order of the day.

Sometimes the subtle little sin called gossip slips into a group's life in the form of a prayer request. The best way for a leader to stop this in its track is to call on James 5:16. "Therefore confess your sins to each other and pray for each other so that you may be healed. The prayer of a righteous man is powerful and effective." The leader needs to lead by reminding the group that the Bible tells us to confess our own faults, not the mess-ups of others. This gives the group a safe place to get real about their own needs. It also helps everyone know the group will not be talking about them when they are absent! Romans 12:16 can also be kept in mind to help a group not to be haughty in their own minds. "Live in harmony with one another. Do not be proud, but be willing to associate with people of low position. Do not be conceited." To stay humble we must remember we are all learners.

Leaders can also lead by example in refusing to pray "siccum" prayers. I am sure you know what I mean. "Siccum" comes from someone who is on the judgment seat, telling God how things are and what He should do to take care of it. Our prayers need to be motivated by love and refuse the temptation to launch missiles!

When we have opportunity to talk to each other in a small group about shortcomings and experience tension because of various inner conflicts, we will hear ourselves saying to them what we ourselves need to hear. I am convinced that these things happen best in the climate of love that God wants a small group to have, not unlike the group Jesus was leading.

A common small group scenario is when someone takes a deep breath and launches into, "I just don't know what to do. My spouse/neighbor/co-worker/boss/child/parent is so _____! He/she _____." Obviously the leader wants to stop it right there, but how? The Jesus way in John 21:22 will help us: "What is that to you? You must follow Me!" When

I have used the Jesus principle to ask, "They aren't here, but you are. How can we pray for you?" I usually get a silent stare in response. It is awkward so I try to help with, "Do you need patience? Do you need wisdom? Do you need courage? Do you need love in your heart? Most of the time I hear a yes with all of the above. Then it is, "Okay, let's pray. Who will lead us as we pray for _____? (the one who brought the request)."

We don't meet together too many times without realizing that group life gets rather messy for us just like it did for the twelve. We are faced with relational problems, either between our members or between one of them and someone not in the group. Please be encouraged to know the **perfect** Jesus did not have a **perfect** group. He teaches us that a kind and gentle spirit can restore peace and harmony where discord has showed itself. Refusing to take sides and refusing to play God will encourage spiritual growth. Stepping up to confront sinful and selfish attitudes will allow a forgiving and cleansing stream to flow in a person's life and in the lives of our small groups.

DISCUSSION QUESTIONS

1. How did Jesus use the conflict in Mark 10:35–41 to teach Kingdom principles in 10:42–45?

2. Name one conflict you have had with a person that resulted in spiritual growth in both of your lives?

3. What are some things a leader can do to make sure their small group is a safe place for people to struggle with the "whatevers" in their lives?

4. Describe a time when you were in a group and did not feel like you measured up to the others who were there. What did you learn that will help you "level the playing field" for people in your small group?

5. How can you help a person in your small group whose level of spiritual maturity has become a problem for others in the group?

Chapter Six

Receiving Deeper Teachings

The gospel of Mark records thirty parables Jesus gave in His public teaching to the general population. But have you noticed He never explained a parable to the crowds? In the small group He was able to give them deeper teaching than He could give the multitudes. More than their eyes and ears and minds, Jesus wanted their hearts. We will discover that instead of prepared lectures, they were able to learn in an interactive, proactive, application-oriented style. More about His teaching style will be discussed in the next chapter.

At times He became weary with their slowness, but He never gave up on them. He knew their words in the future would be empty and their conviction would be shaky unless they could have their questions answered by the Master Teacher. To me this means more than just being in a huge auditorium or stadium with a great teacher. True, a person might say they have been with So-and-So, but Jesus wanted to give the twelve more than what He could give a crowd.

In my own small group ministry, I have tried to adopt the Jesus way to connect the apostolic teaching in a large group to the personal application of those truths in a small group setting. Here is how it has worked in a very practical way:

- God inspires and anoints the pastor/teacher in the congregation with the Scripture He wants to be proclaimed.
- A few discussion questions are then prepared from the Scripture text, not from the sermon. An application-oriented sample is on page 92–93.
- The Word of God is preached in an atmosphere of awe-inspiring worship.
- The facilitator/leader of the small group makes a copy of the prepared discussion guide (not a lesson) available to each one in the group as they arrive.
- Without requiring homework, everyone in the group is able to interact with the Scripture text, whether they have heard the sermon or not.
- Accountability is the natural follow-up to commitments made in the group to integrate the truth into daily life.

Several years ago I made a list of the benefits I had found in using this simple system instead of having each small group choose for itself a guide for this dialogue. I was surprised at how many advantages eventually came to my attention when I started writing them down. (Appendix B)

Before we look at specific occasions when Jesus gave the twelve deeper explanations of what they had just heard in the large group setting, we need to clarify the role He was assuming. This will help us follow Jesus, our small group leader.

His role as a "teacher" with the twelve was more like a mentor or sponsor than a stand-up-in-front teacher with all the answers. How many people has God entrusted to your care who need encouragement and insight from you to be able to put his truth into their daily lives? The relationship between disciple and discipler is motivated and sustained with a mutual, reciprocated love. Besides the sharing of knowledge, there is ample opportunity to pray, weep, laugh and work together. The modeling of your concern and your care is the most transferable part of being a discipler in a small group. And remember, your objective is to help them to each become a disciple of Jesus Christ, not a disciple of yourself. Don't try to be the whole body of Christ. Be faithful to do your part and allow others to do theirs so the persons you are with will be transformed into the likeness of Christ. The small group has a vital role in shaping and molding the deeper parts of each person's life in Christ.

The joy of "making disciples" in a small group comes because we are giving life to our people, not just information. It gets the process out of academia. When the mentor, Paul, was helping people solve their life issues, he never separated doctrine from real life. He taught them to deal with their sins and shortcomings in the context of their daily lives and relationships. It can be called "just-in-time" learning. It is the way parents teach (day by day, week after week, month after month, year after year), applying ageless principles in real-life situations. That means we don't have to prepare a three- to six-month course of study. We follow the Sunday teaching each week with a discussion guide that is application-focused. The depth of teaching is for the **doing** more than the knowing.

As our three children moved from our home to establish homes of their own I soon discovered that my parenting continued. We still share significant life with each other. I mention this here because it provides a helpful analogy for the relationship that continues strong after a group has commissioned leaders to go to create a new group. But that whole process is reserved for a later chapter.

AWAY FROM THE CROWD

By way of illustration we need to see a few occasions when Jesus seized the moment to do a deeper teaching. It seems that when He was most popular, when the momentum had definitely shifted His way, He needed more time away by Himself and with the twelve. Not all of the teaching was explaining parables and Kingdom pictures. Oh, so many times I have wished we had more of the table conversations about what someone said and how it was said. Or the casual chatter about the fishing season and the wholesale price of bass and perch. Or even a sample or two of their jokes ("Have you heard the one about the Roman soldier who walked into this little village and…").

Mark's fourth chapter is filled with parables. In verses 4:10–11, "When he was alone, the twelve and the others around him asked him about the parables. He told them, "The secret of the kingdom of God has been given to you. But to those on the outside everything is said in parables," and in 4:33–34 we know He went over everything He had been teaching the crowds. "With many similar parables Jesus spoke the word to them, as much as they could understand. He did not say anything to them without using a parable. But when he was alone with his own disciples, he explained everything." He was untying the knots and smoothing out the tangles in their understanding. They needed this to be able to draw from it later.

In Mark 8:10–21 the evidence of His being the Messiah was all around them, but they were slow to receive it. They were finding fault with each other about who forgot to bring the bread. Jesus gets into the discussion to teach them about not being like the Pharisees. Verse 8:21 in the Message translation is such a disappointing one for the Lord when He says, "Do you still not get it?"

Peter, James and John discussed what they had experienced on the mountain in Mark 9 as they walked back down into the real world. They were trying to find the meaning in the midst of all the dazzle. When the four of them got back to the other nine, they found them surrounded with a crowd accusing them of failing in their ministry. Jesus was weary of their slowness (9:19), but He did not give up on them. "O unbelieving generation," Jesus replied, "how long shall I stay with you?" How long shall I put up with you? He did not give in to His feelings of disappointments. He healed the lunatic boy and continued teaching.

Before going back into Jerusalem, Jesus takes the twelve where He had been baptized and where he had recruited His first disciples. He was teaching them about surrendering some things as important as marriage and money (Mark 10:1–31). In a bragging tone Peter asks a question. Jesus encouraged him (and them) by reviewing what their rewards would be and then humbled him (and them) by saying that right motives would be the key. He wanted us to know that if we try to pull it off by ourselves, we fail. But if we let God do it there is no limit to what can be accomplished. Unexpected issues will appear as we do our ministry, but our Lord continues to teach us as we seize every teachable moment the Holy Spirit gives us to help our small group members to grow up in their faith.

When we arrive at Mark 10:31, it seems Jesus does the summary of this teaching with wild sweeping gestures: "But many who are first will be last, and the last first." Again, He seems to be talking to them as a parent to his children. He wanted them to know that God sees the intentions of the heart. The ones who are promoting themselves to be first will be last. Those who are generous and self-forgetful will be first.

On their way into Jerusalem (about ten days before his death), Jesus again calls the twelve aside and for the third time He tells them what to expect (Mark 10:32–45). Luke 18:34 says they still did not understand what He was saying. "The disciples did not understand any of this. Its meaning was hidden from them, and they did not know what he was talking about." In their confusion, James and John made their presumptuous and selfish request. Jesus did not pounce on them with hurtful words. He responded as a loving parent to a child who has brought a senseless request. He continued to teach the ten offended ones that the way He prescribed was not the way of the Gentiles who lord it over others. This seemed to settle them down.

After visiting the Temple the last time and chasing the cheating businessmen from their tables, he went to the Mount of Olives.

> As he was leaving the temple, one of his disciples said to him, "Look, Teacher! What massive stones! What magnificent buildings!" "Do you see all these great buildings?" replied Jesus. "Not one stone here will be left on another; every one will be thrown down." As Jesus was sitting on the Mount of Olives opposite the temple, Peter, James, John and Andrew asked him privately, "Tell us, when will these things happen? And what will be the sign that they are all about to be fulfilled?" (Mark 13:1–4)

On His way with four of the twelve, they were admiring the massive Temple stones. Jesus said they would all be thrown down and they wondered when and how. It was another private opportunity for Him to give them a deeper teaching about the end of the age.

One more illustration is found in Mark 14:22–25.

> While they were eating, Jesus took bread, gave thanks and broke it, and gave it to his disciples, saying, "Take it; this is my body." Then he took the cup, gave thanks and offered it to them, and they all drank from it. "This is my blood of the covenant, which is poured out for many," he said to them. "I tell you the truth, I will not drink again of the fruit of the vine until that day when I drink it anew in the kingdom of God."

Not only does Jesus observe the Passover meal with them, but He uses the event to teach them more about His death. He was trying to help them see His cross as being redemptive. Since blood gives life, they would know that His crucifixion was not a fatal blow. His body would be given—given, not taken. His blood would be poured out for them and for us! Jesus uses another common experience (Passover) to teach the deeper truths. This is the same dynamic we experience when we open ourselves the open Bible and let the Holy Spirit make application of its truth to our daily lives. It is a dangerous thing to own a Bible and know how to read! And because of the dialogue with each other with our Bibles open, we not only receive helpful insight, but also encouragement with accountability to obey God's voice—encouragement and accountability that doesn't happen in a large group.

THE POWER OF DIALOGUE

For years I have been influenced by a statement I received somewhere and have passed it on many times without remembering how it came to me: "Dialogue is to a relationship what blood is to the body...there is no life without it."

Putting this now into the context of small group life which is built primarily with relationships, we quickly see how important it is to remove all barriers which would hinder dialogue. How does a small group become a **community of believers**? Answer: When the members enter into dialogue with one another and assume responsibility for their common life. It is the giving and receiving of life, the life of Christ. However, we know from time to time some people say what they want to say without regard to the others in the group. This is called monologue. Extended monologue in a small group does not take other people seriously; does not value them and/or their thoughts and feelings. In the community of believers, we all need both affirmation and correction by our brothers and sisters. How can living faith be passed from one person to another, one family to another, unless it has a direct encounter through a shared life?[1]

This is also an important lesson for a small group leader who lives with two temptations: (1) to impose his/her own opinions and force the group to either obey or rebel or do nothing and (2) to give no direction whatever in the name of freedom. Information **must** be passed along, but unless it is related to life it is just more stuff without much meaning.

Jesus modeled for the twelve and for us the kind of dialogue where honest communication and learning can take place; not only on an intellectual level, but on an emotional level as well. Notice again how many times anger, fear, love, courage, et cetera. were expressed as the disciples talked to each other. A healthy small group has a trust climate that provides safety and security when emotions are expressed. Participating in this kind of dialogue makes it possible for masks to be left outside the meeting place. Ideas and feelings, confessions and commitments flow easily in this environment.

God brought a very special friend into my life in 1976 who pastored a church that planted "Home Bible Classes" all over the west side of Portland, Oregon. Pastor Albert Wollen at the Cedar Mill Bible Church helped me understand the way the large group events complimented and were in turn complimented by the small "family groups."

Pastor Wollen will never know how much I learned from him that has influenced me to this present day—even though I have tried to tell him. A few of those nuggets I have endeavored to put into my ministry through the years with small group leaders are:

- God honors His Word and so it needs to be allowed to enter into a group's dialogue. The Bible will speak for itself if we let it.
- A group is led by a concerned and compassionate person who does not see himself/herself as some kind of spiritual therapist. The leader is a learner.
- A leader can only know the group has heard what he/she has tried to say if they are given opportunity to talk back! It is called dialogue.
- The mechanics of group life will fail if there is no enthusiasm in what is happening. Let the Holy Spirit inspire and motivate.
- Instead of thinking lesson material, think life. The focus is on how the group shares with each other in encouraging/edifying ways.
- Leaders lead with I-messages rather than "they say" and "we believe." By being honest and vulnerable the leader stays on a personal level with his/her group.

The New Testament is written in such **relational** words: older men are called fathers, older women are treated as mothers, younger men and women are brothers and sisters. These relationships provide a framework for a caring ministry that cannot function unless there is a primary place for dialogue. When my wife and I were raising our family it was most often at our kitchen table. If our ministry is based on monologue, then we can hardly expect the New Testament spirit of **family** to be the testimony of our church.[2] Dialogue is one of the best things that happens when a group comes together. As people arrive, they immediately start telling stories to each other. And then when we dialogue with the Lord in conversational prayer and in the discussion of His Word, the spoken words become the servants of the Holy Spirit in the hearts of the group's members. "Then those who feared the LORD talked with each other, and the Lord listened and heard" (Malachi 3:16).

Dialogue flows easily in a safe place, where the words don't have to be weighed or calculated. Each person enters into dialogue for the purpose of gaining understanding and insight, not just to give some. It could be that we offer what we think is a great idea and realize we are totally alone with it. Does that mean we never speak up again and never take a stand on anything? No, we just know that even if we might be in the minority on a subject, we are not alienated from the people God has brought into our lives. And if we share an off-the-wall opinion that is just wacky, our group will raise their eyebrows, but they will still love us!

The element of trust is fundamental to dialogue. Without trust, a group is only playing a little game. Trust is developed with time and patience in which the leader leads the way by sharing some challenges from his/her own life. It is okay for trust to stay at a somewhat shallow level until the reliability of the group is proven.[3] We must keep in mind that we all have things to learn from whomever God brings into our group. Each of us also has something wonderful to share from our Lord Jesus that will build others up, too!

APPLICATION IS THE DESTINATION

The twelve needed time away to dialogue so they could start applying into their lives what they learned. Jesus was teaching them a "doing gospel." If they needed some time away in a small group to find ways to "do the gospel," so do we.

My wife and I had the privilege of being with a tour group in Western Turkey and Greece, following the steps of the Apostle Paul. This was a deep desire of mine for many years—to visit the cities where Paul brought the Good News out of Jerusalem to non-Jews like me. I was asked to lead our devotion time in Miletus where Paul reviewed his ministry in Ephesus (Acts 20:18–21) with the elders who had come to say goodbye to him.

> When they arrived, he said to them: "You know how I lived the whole time I was with you, from the first day I came into the province of Asia. I served the Lord with great humility and with tears, although I was severely tested by the plots of the Jews. You know that I have not hesitated to preach anything that would be helpful to you but have taught you publicly and from house to

house. I have declared to both Jews and Greeks that they must turn to God in repentance and have faith in our Lord Jesus.

Earlier that day we had already visited the ancient city of that healthy Ephesian church. We learned how a population of 250,000 was filled with pagan gods and goddesses and such a mixture of various ethnic groups. We also learned about the great success God had given them to turn huge numbers toward Christ by the faithful ministry of the believers. How did they reach their city? Acts 20:20 has the super simple key: they were taught publicly daily for two years and they were discipled in their homes. Does that sound a bit familiar? Yes, because that is exactly how Jesus had modeled the reproducible system. Public teaching and then application with accountability in his small group. Let's follow the Leader. Paul did. John Wesley did. Pastor Cho does.

Sermons are monologues by design and small groups promote dialogue by design. By having a few discussion questions that lead to application of the biblical truth that has been taught, the large group and the small group get connected. There is no substitute for the small group's ability to dialogue. The following is a sample discussion guide that is written so that full participation is possible beginning with the very first two questions. Then questions 3–6 are written to allow the Bible to speak for itself as it enters into the dialogue. Question 7 is the commitment one in which each person can state his/her part in a measurable goal.

PUTTING LOVE INTO ACTION

1. What are some things a person can do to let you know he or she really cares for you?

2. What are some things that cause you trouble in your relationships with your friends and family?

3. Read Romans 12:9–13. In the first part of verse nine, what is the high-priority quality the Apostle Paul says love must have? In the second part of that same verse, Paul tells us to do what?

4. When conflicts and problems arise between two people, how can this scriptural truth be put into practice?

5. Read verse 12:10 in unison from The Living Bible, "Love each other with brotherly affection and take delight in honoring each other." What are some ways to honor people who are younger than you? Those who are your age? Those who are older?

6. Read verses 12:11–13 again. Of the commands listed in these three verses, which **two** are the easiest for you to keep? Which **one** seems to be the most difficult to keep?

7. Before our next meeting, how can each of us put love into action in our homes, our places of employment, neighborhoods, and so on? Let's be specific: "I can put my love into action by…"

In order for us to be able to do the "deeper teaching" like Jesus did with His small group, there are two very practical things that need to be present. The first is an experience many of us have endured in a small group when the discussion was dry and not at all stimulating even though our Bibles were open. How can a Bible discussion be dry?

- It could be because of not having been given the chance to apply its truth to daily life.

- It could be because the questions were closed.

By that I mean they were correctly answered yes or no or they were answered correctly from the verse we just read. When our goal is to lead a group toward dialogue, we need to create questions that are open for discussion and not closed with a correct answer. Open questions are stimulating and bring life to a group and keep it moving forward.

Another common experience in a group is an academic emphasis on understanding what the Bible says. Obviously we must know what God says before we can apply it in real life situations, but our goal is transformation more than information. God wants His Word to get a grip on our hearts! Having our minds stimulated with new thoughts is a wonderful experience for all of us. But perhaps a better closing question for every group meeting could be, "How do you think God wants to change you or our group with what we have been discussing?" Our goal is make sure every group member leaves with something to feel, to remember, to do.[4] That is the deeper teaching Jesus modeled for us.

LET'S FOLLOW THE LEADER!

Receiving Deeper Teachings

DISCUSSION QUESTIONS

1. Jesus loved to teach with real life stories, such as Mark 4:1–9. But what are some of the reasons He couldn't do the "deeper teaching" (4:10–20) with the crowds—only with His small group?

2. How did Jesus use the Passover Meal with His small group (Mark 14:12–26) to teach them some unforgettable lessons?

3. How will the way we discuss the scriptures in our small group make a difference for God in their daily lives?

4. In your opinion, what is the difference between being in a class and being in a small group? Between teaching a class and leading a small group?

5. Which of the two will multiply quicker in the life of a church, a class or a small group? Why?

Chapter Seven

LEARNING HIS TEACHING STYLE

Even though Jesus was a Master Teacher, He loved the opportunities to interact with the twelve. His desire was for them to discover truth for themselves, not just to be told the truth. He also wanted them to be able to not only teach **what** He had taught, but I believe He wanted them to do it in the same **way**—in small groups. It was a reproducible teaching style.

In the early months when they were with Him, they were not sent out to teach, only to announce the good news of God's Kingdom being right where they were. They were to proclaim that the Kingdom of God was available. All they had to do was trust this man, Jesus, the Anointed One. As His apprentices in our own faith journey, we get to do the same announcing of the good news today.

Jesus was careful to watch for familiar objects in order to teach eternal truths. Some of these include: soil, light, corn, seeds, sparrows, ravens, trees, branches, sheep and goats. Do you remember how He taught a valuable lesson with a child on his lap? A coin in His hand? Do you see his reproducible method of making reference to a water pot, a wine skin, lighting a lamp, the widow's mite, catching fish and constructing a house? He used current issues and daily chores to make eternal truth come alive. Let's follow the Leader.

When He did commission them to "go and teach," He made it clear that they were to do it in the same way He had done it with them—namely, that God's will is accomplished in the ordinary events of daily life. They were to teach in the context of what had actually happened to them more than lofty ideals from a faraway course of study. They were to draw from both the old and the new treasures of their own lives (Matthew 13:52): "He said to them, 'Therefore every teacher of the law who has been instructed about the kingdom of heaven is like the owner of a house who brings out of his storeroom new treasures as well as old'" When the day came for them to hear the assignment in Mark 16:15 and Matthew 28:18–20, they knew exactly what He had in mind because of what they had experienced with Him. If Jesus would have been an eloquent speaker or a skilled lecturer, not many (if any) could have followed that kind of lead.

Jesus patiently explained the parables to the twelve so He could mold/shape their character. They shared life with each other so they could see the integration of His training and doing. Thus they were learning how to be disciple-makers! Not just because they now knew Him, but because they had become like Him.[1] Who are the ones in your life who are not only serving the Lord because of your ministry, but who are discipling someone else to be like Jesus?

Discipling is hard work. Training is harder than telling. That is because to disciple a person requires an investment of our lives. "We loved you so much that we were delighted to share with you not only the gospel of God but our lives as well, because you had become so dear to us" (1 Thessalonians 2:8). When we share Christ we are giving away His life, not just more information about His life. We are also giving away **our** lives. God wants our small groups to interact with our culture by listening, learning and sharing. We need to go where the people are because they do not always show up at our church on Sunday morning! We must realize they are unconnected from God and the church, but have deep desires to be changed, rather than to belong:

To be whole, rather than be safe;
To be free, rather than to be rooted;

To be mentored, rather than to be lectured;
To be vindicated, rather than to be corrected;
To be destined, rather than to be saved.[2]

In order for our small groups to be redemptive in meeting people where they are and then help them become all God wants them to be, we must get them involved in meaningful dialogue. Good questions provoke thought and stimulate learning and growth. Jesus, as a small group leader, asked lots of questions. Someone took the time to count approximately 154 questions Jesus asked in the gospels. By looking at those, we find various types of questions which can lead our people toward life change.

Personal: What have you been struggling with lately? What is it you need God's help with? If you had been there, what would you have done? Can you see yourself doing this? Why or why not?

Background: Where else does this appear in the Bible?

Application: What is God saying to you in this passage? What do you think the next step will be for you? What small step can you take in this direction this next week?

These are only samples, but you can quickly see how they can lead a group to not be "hearers only."

Jesus also loved to use stories to help His listeners to understand the principles of the Kingdom of God. Telling stories and using allegories and other illustrations were His primary ways of communicating truth from God to mankind. He used the stories from their familiar surroundings and the events of their lives to help them understand truths which were not yet familiar to them. His stories got their attention and kept it. They helped to further explain something He had already given them. Sometimes His entire lesson was in story form. He also wanted them to be able to place Old Testament scriptures alongside popular assumptions in order to test the validity of practices which were common in their culture.

Mark chapter ten gives us a good illustration of this teaching style as Jesus tells the story of the rich young leader who chose his riches instead of following after God. The culture thought if someone had wealth it was because of God's favor. Now Jesus was explaining how the heart was where the young man should have been giving his attention, not to whether he was rich or poor. Jesus wanted the disciples to go and teach in such a way to bring about transformation in the lives who listened to them, not only to dispense helpful information to those who would listen. Jesus wanted to do more than be the big "jug" pouring words into all the little empty "mugs." He deeply desired to make a significant impact in the lives of the twelve, whether they took notes or not! We just automatically remember those things that make a difference in our lives.

I did not have a notebook with me in the summer of 1959 when I had a heart to heart conversation with my pastor in Lincoln, Nebraska, but I will never forget what I learned while standing with him out in front of that church building. Nor did I have a notebook with me to take notes of what was happening when I heard the news on my car radio that President John F. Kennedy had been shot in Dallas, Texas. I was on my way to do some business at a bank and was so shocked in disbelief I stayed in my car in the parking lot for almost an hour. It was in the spring of 1980 and I was living in Portland, Oregon, when Mt. St. Helens blew its top. I will never forget what I experienced that day, even though I did not take notes and have a written test later so my learning could be measured.

My life has been impacted by experiences such as these three instances which came along in the flow of life. Master teachers are able to impact our lives for the simple fact that we were with them. The lessons we have learned from them beyond the words continue long after the teacher has finished the teaching.

A few years ago I was impacted by Dallas Willard's book, *The Divine Conspiracy*. It is not a book about small groups, per se, but Willard makes the point very clear that transformation of the heart needs to be our primary objective. Special experiences, faithfulness in church attendance, correct doctrine and all external conformity do not (in themselves) produce transformation. The human heart needs to be plowed much deeper. These things (as important as they are) only burden the soul and make significant Chirstlikeness extremely difficult.[3]

The training of a disciple that leads to obedience must disrupt the old self-oriented patterns. We must go beyond simply telling the old nature not to bother us. The twelve steps of AA are designed to change the destructive patterns in a person's life and help him/her become free from whatever has him/her bound. The first four help them know their need of God, but the other eight cannot be neglected. They are designed to help a person live and grow stronger in their freedom. The twelve steps are a lifetime spiritual journey we all need to incorporate into our lives. Step number one has to be number one or we never will start! That is the step where I admit I have a problem. Step two is where I admit I cannot solve this on my own. Step three is recognizing I need God's help. Now I am on my way! The old patterns are being put away so the new ones can get strong and healthy. You see it is more than knowing truth. It is *doing* truth intentionally that transforms a person's inner life.

THE CONTRAST WITH OTHER TEACHERS

The words of Christ in the Sermon on the Mount stop at Matthew 7:27, but we cannot neglect to read the brief comment Matthew gives in verses 7:28–29. He says the people were amazed because His teaching was so different than the other teachers of the law. What was so unique? Matthew adds the comment that Jesus taught with authority, like a parent who gives instruction to a child and fully expects the child to take action. Evidently the other teachers gave out teachings and more teachings, whether the people put it into their lives or not. Jesus expected a commitment to make the application or their lives would only be like a building a house on sand (Matthew 7:26).

You see, Jesus did not just teach content. He gave to them of Himself. He knew they needed more than a heaven-sent dispenser of information. They needed **Him**. He wanted them to respond to a God who loved them, not just when they obeyed the law. The God of the Bible was (is) a God who desired (desires) a relationship with His people. In the same way, He then wanted them to give of themselves to others.

Jesus taught them that the nature of God is love. Love freely gives itself away. They were learning to be disciple-makers by giving themselves to others: "Greater love has no one than this, that he lay down his life for his friends" (John 15:13). I call it: **loving people God's way**. This would be the only way they could understand what would happen at the cross that Friday afternoon after Passover. He told them in Matthew 10:8 to give away what they had received—LIFE, abundant and eternal. "Heal the sick, raise the dead, cleanse those who have leprosy, drive out demons. Freely you have received, freely give." Obviously we cannot give away what we don't have. And when we give it, it proves that we indeed possess it.

Perhaps the twelve could not always understand **why** Jesus did what He did, but they could not help but know **what** He was doing. His very life was an unmistakable witness of who God was and what He expected of them. To illustrate this we turn to the story of how John discovered a man (unknown to them) who was casting out devils in the name of Jesus.

> "Teacher," said John, "we saw a man driving out demons in your name and we told him to stop, because he was not one of us." "Do not stop him," Jesus said. "No one who does a miracle in my name can in the next moment say anything bad about me, for whoever is not against us is for us. I tell you the truth, anyone who gives you a cup of water in my name because you belong to Christ will certainly not lose his reward." (Mark 9:38–41)

The beloved disciple tried to make it appear that the man was suspect because he was not one of their tight little circle. Perhaps they had enjoyed a monopoly use of God's power and wanted to keep it that way. However, one thing is clear: They were willing to be instructed. They were honest in what they had done and in what they wanted to learn. This makes it possible for Jesus to forthrightly state, "Do not stop him…for he who is not against us is for us."[4]

I am so glad that Mark 8:27–30 is reported in order for us to have a window into the life of this small group of twelve with their Leader: "Jesus and his disciples went on to the villages around Caesarea Philippi. On the way he asked them, '"Who do people say I am?' They replied, 'Some say John the Baptist; others say Elijah; and still others, one of the prophets.' 'But what about you?' he asked. 'Who do you say I am?' Peter answered, 'You are the Christ.' Jesus warned them not to tell anyone about him."

As they traveled together, Jesus asked them to tell Him what they had been hearing as they had associated with people regarding their opinions of Him. He knew that people were probably more inclined to talk to them than to Him. When He heard their answers, there is no debate reported. He only turned to them and asked, "Who do you say I am?"

Jesus quickly and gladly accepted Peter's reply and gave him credit for speaking the words of God that were beyond himself. He blessed Peter and promised that the church would be built on that kind of confession of faith.

Do you see how this small group leader set the stage for them to participate in their own learning? The learning happened in a reproducible dialogue style. He asked open-ended questions which were directed toward the truth of who He was. He wanted to be sure that fact was established in their minds without just telling them again what He had already told them. Peter knew the truth because he could give it. We can do the same with the small group we lead:

- As we give ourselves along with scriptural truth.
- As we ask open-ended questions to determine how our people are doing with their faith journey.
- As we use stories that get to the heart of the matter.

THE INDUCTIVE METHOD

Jesus chose to examine truth and then apply it to life rather than settle on a premise and then try to get the scriptures to prove it to be true. That would be a deductive method. The student of God's Word today has a great variety of resources to help him/her know what it says. But those should only be used to help with the application of the truth revealed already in the student's diligent study. In short, the process of induction is used to establish truth; the process of deduction is used to yield the implications of that truth for life application.

Jesus promised that part of the Holy Spirit's job description was to guide us into all truth. "But when he, the Spirit of truth, comes, he will guide you into all truth. He will not speak on his own; he will speak only what he hears, and he will tell you *what is yet to come.*" (John 16:13 Emphasis added) He is faithful to shine God's light on a passage of Scripture so we can apply it. The Holy Spirit will re-speak the written words until they become the living words from God to us. It is very much like a scientific method where He helps us discover the facts concerning a matter before we start drawing up our conclusions. Upon visiting a physician the first time, the facts of our situation are gathered before a treatment program is designed to get us back to health.[5]

In the life of a small group it is important to open our Bibles and allow God's Word to speak for itself. Then (and only then) are we ready to draw up a plan to put the truth into our lives. The leader facilitates the learning process, acknowledging that Jesus is the One who speaks truth. Learning to lead the dialogue is a skill that must be developed like any other skill. (i.e.: typing, driving, athletic competition, music, etc.). Practice. Practice. Practice. God will bless every effort we make to help our group "hear from Heaven."

THE REPRODUCIBLE METHOD

I have realized while writing a few of these thoughts that it is very difficult to pinpoint the fact that Jesus actually had a method. It is difficult for us to imagine how Jesus could be so successful and not give us an idea about successful techniques. Oh, how many times I have wished we had His small group leader's how-to manual right here in our hands. Or a manual with the basic steps, 1-2-3-4-5, to lead an unbeliever to life-changing faith in Christ.

Jesus did have a method and He was it! He did with them what He expected them to learn. They saw Him relate to all kinds of people with all kinds of needs. He won their confidence, announced that the way to God was through Him and then called them to make a decision. I guess we might call this the **natural** way.[6]

It has been several years now since that happy day when I became a grandfather. My grandchildren have added so much joy to my life! A big part of that joy is the joy I have with their parents, my children. When I watch them parent their children, I am so encouraged. I see them parenting so much better than I was ever able to do with them. Yes, I am proud of them. I ask myself how it is possible for them to do so well and they have never been to "Parent's School?" Well, I do know that they are depending on God to help them with the choices they have daily in their families. But I also know that they had parents who loved them through those formative years. We endeavored to train them, not just tell them. We knew someday our success in parenting would be determined by how well they did away from us. So far as I can see today, their "methods" are very similar to our "methods." Not perfect, but reproducible nevertheless.

I am suggesting to you that there is no higher calling than to reproduce the character of Christ in another person. Jesus expects each of us to bear spiritual fruit. "I am the vine; you are the branches. If a man remains in me and I in him, he will bear much fruit; apart from me you can do nothing" (John 15:5). The Apostle Paul told the Thessalonians that **they** were his glory and joy.[7] "For what is our hope, our joy, or the crown in which we will glory in the presence of our Lord Jesus when he comes? Is it not you? Indeed, you are our glory and joy" (1 Thessalonians 2:19–20). And then in 2 Timothy 2:2, he says that we are to teach others what we have received in such a way that they in time can pass it on to others. "And the things you have heard me say in the presence of many witnesses entrust to reliable men who will also be qualified to teach others." When this happens, the life transforming power of God's grace continues to be multiplied.

Years ago I was asked to return to a church where I had pastored to assist with a funeral for a person who had been a small group leader when I was there. While sitting on the platform and looking around to see how many I could recognize, I suddenly realized there were at least eight people who were leading small groups after they had been in John and

Helen's group. When it came time for me to give personal words, I was so thrilled to announce what I had just observed. Her faithful ministry was outliving her own life because she gave it away. She was following her Leader!

LEARNING HIS TEACHING STYLE

DISCUSSION QUESTIONS

1. Jesus loved to tell stories. How is it that story telling is still a very effective way to communicate eternal truth?

2. How does Jesus letting the four disciples ask questions (Mark 13:1+) open them for some real learning to take place?

3. Read again the confession of Peter in Matthew 16:13–20. Notice Jesus did not ask yes or no (closed) questions. What were they (verses 16:13 and 15)? What does this tell us about the teaching style of their Leader?

4. What are some of the many benefits the author lists for discussion guides to be prepared for small group leaders from the scripture the pastor used in teaching the people in the large group?

5. Name a leader who has influenced you and has made a big difference in your life with Christ. What did you receive from him/her that you want to imitate with those you have opportunity to lead?

Chapter Eight

SENDING THEM OUT

On the night before His death, Jesus said that the disciples would do greater things than they had seen Him do in the time He had been with them. "I tell you the truth, anyone who has faith in me will do what I have been doing. He will do even greater things than these, because I am going to the Father" (John 14:12). His instruction was clear and simple: the Holy Spirit would make them able to heal, raise the dead and cast out devils in His name. They were to preach repentance and welcome the Kingdom of God.

The biblical method was and is to make disciples with an apprentice system to raise up more disciples who will do the same. Jesus recruited the twelve with a life development vision. He looked beyond their status at the beginning to their full potential in the future, knowing it would take time to form attitudes, values and skills. He knew that to get faith out of them He needed to demonstrate faith in them.

In a small group where we get to share life on a regular basis, we can testify that these people very soon become like family to us. We trust each other. We pray for each other. We laugh, cry, study, work, sing, eat, worship and celebrate together…like family. And part of family life is to "raise 'em up and send 'em out!" In Psalm 127:3–5 we discover that our children are like arrows in the quiver.

Sons are a heritage from the LORD,
children a reward from him.
Like arrows in the hands of a warrior
are sons born in one's youth.
Blessed is the man
whose quiver is full of them.
They will not be put to shame
when they contend with their enemies in the gate.

That is a great analogy also for us in this context, because arrows are not designed to stay in the quiver! Their purpose is to be ready on call to be sent. Part of the prayer of our Lord in the garden was telling his Heavenly Father that He had completed the assignment He had been given (John 17:4). Completed, as in finished? Obviously the whole world had not come to repentance, and many villages still had hurting people who needed His healing touch. But He was convinced the eleven could be successful doing **His** ministry after He was ascended into heaven. His "arrows" were soon to be released from the quiver and placed in the bow of the Holy Spirit.

In order to go and "make disciples" they first of all needed to be disciples. In this there is no mystery. To be a disciple (or apprentice) of Jesus is something that is easily identified by the evidence of a person's life. Sometimes there are those who claim to be Christian, but their lives do not have the distinguished marks of a disciple—which is living Jesus' way. We do not have access to the books of heaven to know if a person is a Christian or not, but we do see whether there is disciple fruit or not by the way they live. Being disciples does not mean we are learning to do "religious things." It really is not just in **what** we do (cook, clerk, CEO, cowboy, chauffeur, clergy), but **how** we do what we do that makes us disciples or not. As disciples we are all in full-time Christian service, speaking and behaving in such a way as it would please the One we follow and serve.

Making disciples for us must be intentional. True followers of Christ do not just suddenly happen to come along. Jesus recruited the willing, devoted, common-type group of twelve so they could see the power of God at work.

He wanted to give them a safe place to grow so they could be better prepared to withstand the storms of life. He helped the twelve to settle their interpersonal relationship problems. The small group gave Him opportunity to do a deeper teaching in such a way that they could go and do the same. And then He took the risk to send them out with His authority and the power of the Holy Spirit.

For centuries the Jews were considered strange because they carried that little wooden chest (The Ark of the Covenant) around with them. They claimed that God was actually with them. Centuries passed and the secret was fully revealed in the coming of our Lord Jesus Christ—God became human. He was Emmanuel, God with us. The Good News is this same God desires to indwell us, too! Now a watching and wondering world wants to know where God is. Announce it today: He is with His people and He is in them. He is available to all who will receive Him.

Just being with Jesus on those dusty roads, by the seashore, in those small villages caused people to experience hope and healing. They felt freer, walked taller, thought nobler, sang more joyfully, lived more abundantly. And that is what still happens when someone encounters the God who is with His people.[1] I am challenging us to go and make a difference. Each of us in our own way can follow the Leader when we keep our Bibles open to know what He did. If we do not know what Jesus did we will probably end up somewhere else!

Jesus fully expected many to believe in Him because of their message and method (John 17:20–23):

> My prayer is not for them alone. I pray also for those who will believe in me through their message, that all of them may be one, Father, just as you are in me and I am in you. May they also be in us so that the world may believe that you have sent me. I have given them the glory that you gave me, that they may be one as we are one: I in them and you in me. May they be brought to complete unity to let the world know that you sent me and have loved them even as you have loved me.

He did not seem to be concerned about the smallness of the beginning. The whole enterprise (cross and resurrection) now depended on their ability to reproduce. He had no other plan than to use the dedicated lives of those who knew Him so well that they were constrained to tell others who would tell others, who would tell others, et cetera.

I am afraid we have tried to do the "going" and the "baptizing" and the "teaching" without giving enough attention and energy to his assignment for disciples to go and make disciples. The Greek text in Matthew 28:19 has one controlling verb: MATHATUSATE. Our goal and purpose is to raise up disciples and we do that by going and baptizing and teaching. Only as disciples are reproduced can the other parts of the Great Commission be fulfilled.[2]

Are you ready for the big test? The big test for each of us as disciples is going to be in the lives of those who follow us. Are we leading them to be Christ-followers and training them to then go and train disciples to do the same? How does a Christian become a disciple? Answer: they are trained by someone who has been trained. Jesus did it in a small group and I am convinced we have the same opportunity.[3]

CLEAR AND SIMPLE INSTRUCTIONS

As we already discovered in the gospel accounts, Jesus had a two-fold purpose when He called the twelve (Mark 3:13–15). He wanted them to be in fellowship with Him and with each other, but also to be ready to go out and represent Him to others. Each of these depends on the other in order to be complete. They were to own the message and to be heralds with His message. They were convinced of the truth they proclaimed, because they had been with Jesus. With confidence and conviction they were sent out very early in their time with Jesus.

By moving a couple of pages to Mark 6:7–13, we see again how Jesus trusted them.

> Calling the Twelve to him, he sent them out two by two and gave them authority over evil spirits. These were his instructions: "Take

nothing for the journey except a staff—no bread, no bag, no money in your belts. Wear sandals but not an extra tunic. Whenever you enter a house, stay there until you leave that town. And if any place will not welcome you or listen to you, shake the dust off your feet when you leave, as a testimony against them." They went out and preached that people should repent. They drove out many demons and anointed many sick people with oil and healed them.

The twelve had been with Him to witness miracles, hearing the teaching about the Kingdom of God, learning how to pray and live. Now they were being sent to evangelize, heal, and minister to the pressing needs that they would encounter. This was to be a growing up time for them. It would also be the highlight for them.

Several years ago I heard a panel of Bible College administrators report the same response from their graduates when asked to share the highlights of their college years. As much as they appreciated the godly faculty members who invested in them, their highlight in the post-graduation interviews was about serving alongside a pastor and being allowed to actually **do** the ministry they only talked about in the classroom.

By looking a little closer at the actual assignment, Jesus told the twelve to start first in the Israeli villages and towns in Galilee. Of course He wanted to reach the entire world, but that would come later. They were not ready yet to deal with a variety of side issues which would be raised by the non-Jewish people groups. Jesus told them they had the power in His name (Mark 6:7–13) to heal the sick, cleanse lepers, raise the dead, cast out devils. They were to preach that the kingdom of heaven was at hand and nothing more, because that was all they really knew! "Repent and get ready for the kingdom!" We say, WOW, Jesus is certainly taking a risk with them. That is true, but it was also a necessary risk.

Even though a huge crowd cheered their return and Herod was aware of their ministry, they did not have much fruit for their labors. In the meantime they were to be enthusiastic as they preached repentance well. Would they face opposition? Yes, but He reminded them that it was Him and His message that was being rejected.

"He who listens to you listens to me; he who rejects you rejects me; but he who rejects me rejects him who sent me." The seventy-two returned with joy and said, "Lord, even the demons submit to us in your name." He replied, "I saw Satan fall like lightning from heaven. I have given you authority to trample on snakes and scorpions and to overcome all the power of the enemy; nothing will harm you. However, do not rejoice that the spirits submit to you, but rejoice that your names are written in heaven." (Luke 10:16–20)

All they had to do was to do His ministry as though He were doing it Himself (whether they wore the little WWJD bracelets or not!).

We cannot overlook the fact that Jesus sent them out two by two. This is a pattern which is followed many times in the Gospels and also through Acts and the Epistles. In eternity, our relational God is three persons in one nature. Therefore we can easily assume that relationships are a high priority with God. Jesus wanted to provide a companionship in ministry for His disciples (the twelve and the seventy).

The small group of disciples were getting started in the active ministry of their Lord—away from Him and on their own (Mark 6:12). It is interesting to notice that as they went out to teach and preach, Jesus went out to do the same (Matthew 11:1)!"[4] After Jesus had finished instructing his twelve disciples, he went on from there to teach and preach in the towns of Galilee." Leaders send and leaders lead.

ACCOUNTABILITY IS ESSENTIAL

I will never forget the afternoon I was trying to find a scripture reference when my eyes landed on Mark 6:30. "The apostles gathered around Jesus and reported to him all they had done and taught." I shouted a loud, "Praise the Lord! I knew that was in there somewhere!" The pastor in the office next to mine could not understand what all the noise was about until I explained. Both of us were trying to supervise the ministry of small group leaders who were not faithful in giving us a brief report of what was happening in their groups. They grumbled often because they did not enjoy the follow-up work of a simple form which could quickly alert us to victory or defeat, success or failure, answers or questions. We were finding it very difficult to fulfill the Ephesians 4:11–13 word to pastors to be coaches. "It was he who gave some to be apostles, some to be prophets, some to be evangelists, and some to be pastors and teachers, to prepare God's people for works of service, so that the body of Christ may be built up until we all reach unity in the faith and in the knowledge of the Son of God and become mature, attaining to the whole measure of the fullness of Christ."

If our leaders wouldn't let us know how they were doing when we couldn't be present to watch over their ministry, then how could we coach them? Now I could let them see that I was asking no more of them than Jesus asked of His disciples, who came back from doing ministry with a report of everything they had **done** and **taught**. Jesus was then able to correct or affirm what had happened so they could go back out and return with an even better report. He would say things like: be watchful, be humble, keep doing it, be generous with grace, be compassionate for the lost and hurting people you meet. This is another one of those areas where I wish we had more of the reporting sessions Jesus had with the twelve and/or the seventy who were sent.

Since the assignment was clear and simple, Jesus was able to follow up with effective accountability. In Mark 16:15-18 we find the huge passing of the responsibility in a rather business-like way.

> He said to them, "Go into all the world and preach the good news to all creation. Whoever believes and is baptized will be saved, but whoever does not believe will be condemned. And these signs will accompany those who believe: In my name they will drive out demons; they will speak in new tongues; they will pick up snakes with their hands; and when they drink deadly poison, it will not hurt them at all; they will place their hands on sick people, and they will get well."

We would probably expect an emotional farewell, but that was not necessary since He was promising that He was not going to ever leave them alone. When He told them to wait for the Holy Spirit, Jesus knew they were good followers and would do what they were instructed to do. The Holy Spirit would also be there to hold them accountable in each mission where they served.

The success of the disciples hinged entirely on how they received the Holy Spirit. Jesus plainly told them to wait in Jerusalem for His coming and only then could they be witnesses to the whole world beginning in Jerusalem. It would be utterly impossible for them (and for us) to accomplish Christ's mission without the "power from on high." Evidently official titles, clerical robes and earned degrees are not required for them to go out to make disciples. These extra things were not forbidden, but would be empty without the power of the Holy Spirit's enabling. The world is changed by ordinary men and women with the power of God's wisdom and God's love and both are communicated with God's enthusiasm.

I know for some of us to enter a discussion about people leaving our small group to help start a new group is very unsettling. So let's let Jesus teach us. Yes, there were no new people added to the twelve because they each needed the growth and preparation for the mission that would soon be given them. As I see it, there might be short periods when a group is closed in order to fulfill their mission of exploding into their world like His group did. My experience has been that spiritual health can only be maintained in a small group if they are open to new life coming in. Sometimes that is in the form of receiving new people; sometimes that is in the releasing of those who are ready to begin a new group.

Of course, the danger is when we decide we must have our needs met before we can open up for the new life to come in. The problem is we will always have needs! Warning: A very toxic self-absorption is easily developed in a group until "the us four and no more" is all that matters to them.

Churches that encourage small groups for the purpose of spiritual growth and fellowship may need to revisit their purpose. God may want us to get open with his grace and reach as many people as we can with the love of Christ. We must continue to reach to each other but must never neglect the outreach to the unreached through open and healthy and multiplying small groups.

Before we wrap up this chapter about the sending ministry of our Leader, let's consider the struggle we all have to limit the number of people, activities and projects we can effectively care for. Did Jesus model a healthy "span of care" in His ministry? Yes, He chose a group of twelve and had an even more intense connection with only three of the twelve. And He was the Son of God!

Some of the practical ways to help ourselves provide healthy boundaries include:

- Make sure you have an apprentice under your span of care who will include some in your small group into their span of care.
- Multiply your group with Spirit-led timing and a natural/healthy strategy.
- Put yourself under a mentor/coach who will encourage you and invest himself or herself into your life.
- Learn how to say no without apology to some good things in order to say yes to other good things.[5]
- Follow the Leader, Jesus, and schedule some time away for yourself. (Mark 6:30-32)

OBVIOUS RESULTS ARE PROMISED

The closing verses in Mark's gospel are filled with hope. Jesus is assuring them that they **will** cast out devils, they **will** speak with new tongues, they **will** lift snakes, they **will** survive if they happen to drink a deadly thing, they will be able to heal the sick. These signs will follow those who believe the message that they proclaim.

We can enjoy the same kind of confidence when we go in the power and the presence of God. The fruit of faithful ministry is in the changed lives of people who go to make other disciple-makers. The decision we need to make is this: Am I going to do ministry or reproduce it?

The following is a dramatic example of what can happen when a group of people operate with mission vision. From 1961 to 1979, M.Y. Chan worked in a night soil pit in China. That meant he spent six to eight hours a day standing in human excrement with no protection, filling buckets with waste to be spread on fields as fertilizer. Not a fun gig. The huge prison camp in Kiangsu province had four main latrine areas, and they all drained into one horrendous hellhole. He stood there every day in sludge sometimes up to his waist. Chan was singled out for this punishment as a Chinese pastor with a church of 300. He survived those eighteen and a half years without one sick day, and his church grew to 5,000 in his absence. Now fifty-eight, he has churches in twenty locations, each with about 1,000 believers.[6]

In the context of a relay race, multiplication of leaders has several requirements: (1) Several passes of the baton must be made; (2) The baton must be passed to the right people; (3) Those who have the baton must pass it on; (4) Every member of the team wins when the final member crosses the finish line.

FOUR WORDS

Since 1986 I have had the joy and the responsibility to coach pastors and church leaders with the vision and strategies for small group ministries. Sometimes the context has been with many churches gathered at a host church with small groups. Sometimes I have led breakout sessions or workshops at a denominational or city-wide conference. Many times it has been a weekend retreat or a two-day seminar with the lay leaders of a local church.

Each time I have finished my presentation with four words. I want to share those with you now with their brief explanations.

WARNING: Keep it simple

For some unknown reason we have a strange tendency in our western culture to complicate simple things. This simplicity is evidenced in our materials, how we train our leaders and how we conduct our meetings.

REMINDER: Let the Holy Spirit do His work

He **will** be active and **will** show us great and mighty things if we **will** depend on Him.

CHALLENGE: Give yourself to a small group

The very best way to discover what God wants to do in a life-giving group is for us to give ourselves to one. Experience for yourself what more books, tapes, DVDs and conferences can never give.

HOPE: That each of us will go out to make disciple-makers

This is one step beyond the words of our Lord to "make disciples." Let's purpose and then stay faithful to the high calling and **Follow our Leader.**

DISCUSSION QUESTIONS

1. The twelve men Jesus recruited (Mark 3:13–19) were called for two reasons (verse 3:14). What were those reasons and how are the two related? How do the two reasons depend on and complete the other?

2. What were the simple instructions Jesus gave His small group in Mark 6:6b–12?

   a. What was the effect of their ministry on the people they touched?

   b. On the opposition movement?

   c. On the disciples themselves?

   d. On Jesus when He heard their reports when they returned?

3. Matthew 9:35–38 tells us Jesus' response when He saw the multitude of people. How did He instruct his small group to pray?

4. When will those prayers (#3) for harvesters ever be answered?

5. List the names of three Christians you want to pray for that they will grow up to be disciple-makers.

Conclusion

The twelve had been with Jesus since they were recruited from the crowd in Mark chapter three. They watched the miracles and participated in them. They heard the teachings and learned how to teach. They prayed and learned how to pray. Through quality time in a variety of experiences they learned how to live in the Kingdom.

It is surprising, however, to see Jesus sending them early in their ministry to towns and villages to evangelize, heal the sick and cast out demons in His name (Mark 6:7–13). Were they ready for this? Our answer would probably be a strong NO. But Jesus saw them as apprentices and this was part of their training. He could not wait for them to do significant ministry away from Him until He was ready to leave. He knew there were needs they could meet in His name when He could not always be with them.

I am convinced that many of us have overtrained our people, and before long they depend on their training instead of on the Lord when they begin their ministry! They would rather come and study how to do ministry than to get out there in the midst of it all. Jesus told them they had freely received, now go and freely give. He did put restrictions on their preaching initially for the simple fact that they did not know much yet! But they were sent anyway. Their prejudices were too strong; they were more Jew than Christian at this point. But they were sent anyway.

The result: Needs were met, miracles happened, fame and crowds followed them. Even Herod's household took note about their making-a-difference ministry (Mark 6:14).

There are two movements in the narrative recorded in Mark's gospel. In this book we have only focused on one—the one I consider the grossly neglected one. The two are:

1) The calling and arousing of the crowds to shake loose from their cold indifference.
2) The training of the twelve.

In the first one, the twelve are the agents; in the second one, they are the center of attention. Which one is the most important in the long term of ministry? I cast my vote with the second one for several reasons.

- It is where Jesus gave His primary energies.
- Teaching (even the kind Jesus did) remains so vague if there is no dialogue for application purposes.
- The lack of public teaching in the first three centuries after Christ did not hinder the church from turning communities right side up.
- Statistics show a startling comparison of those brought to faith in Christ with those who have been raised up in their faith. (Re: Appendix E)

There is a simplicity in raising up believers in "spiritual families" like it was done in the first century church. Not in the crowds, because the "one-to-anothers" can not be done in crowds. For example, "How do you love a crowd"? We love each other in small groups where we get to do life together, where we experience the give and take of life—the successes and failures, the joys and sorrows. According to 1 John 4:7, God wants us to practice those valuable lessons in family groups as we have opportunity to interact with each other.

It is in the "spiritual family" where assignments are given to "children" who are not yet responsible so they will become responsible. That is where mistakes are made, questions asked both ways: "Dad, what do I do about this?" "Well, what are our options?" Then, "Which of those would be the best?" "Okay, I think that's a good thing, too. I'll help you with it." I truly believe God is calling us to grow His church the way He first designed it and how His Son modeled it for us.

First Peter 2:5 has always received special attention from me because I am a pastor by calling and a stone mason by trade. I have laid up walls and fireplaces with cut or dimension stone, but my favorite is to use rubble—pieces large and small, all shapes and sizes and colors. It is a challenge to try to make something beautiful from a pile of broken stones where no two are the same, but I love it! Peter says we are to be "living stones" fit together into a spiritual house.

Years ago we had out-of-town guests visit our Sunday morning worship gathering. Before entering the auditorium, the wife commented about how noisy the place was with clusters of friendly people everywhere. It was so different than their home church where people tended to stay to themselves because they did not really know each other. When we had lunch later we had an opportunity to talk about the contrast she experienced. That is when we realized it was because the large majority of our people were "living stones" that were experiencing life in a spiritual family each week and they were excited to be together again for worship. Their church back home had "living stones" that were still lying in a pile waiting to be fit together.

POSTSCRIPT

It is a somewhat empty feeling to have Mark's gospel end at verse 16:8, but does it? "Trembling and bewildered, the women went out and fled from the tomb. They said nothing to anyone, because they were afraid." By the evidence we have, that's where Mark left it. Others added the other verses after they read Matthew, Luke and John and felt as we do that now it is more complete. It needed a proper closing.[1]

However, let me suggest that I think it is okay to end at verse 16:8 if we are determined to **follow the Leader**, so those who follow us in future generations will also follow the Leader. In that way the gospel has no end! Mark could tell us where the gospel begins but he could not tell us where it would end.

CONCLUSION

DISCUSSION QUESTIONS

1. Discuss the Jesus training strategy. How is our small group ministry the same and how is it different?

2. When Mark's gospel ends at 16:8, does it seem "unfinished"? What is the best way we can finish writing about the Good News of Jesus in our own ministry?

3. How has the division of clergy and laity hindered our ability to follow the Great Commission Jesus gave us? What can be done to bridge the gap and "make disciples"?

4. What are some assignments you might give a new Christian to help him/her grow up in their faith?

    i. Early in his/her walk with the Lord?

    ii. Later in his/her walk with the Lord?

5. **Do the math:** Congratulations! You are being sent to evangelize a county of 2500 people. In that county, 1800 live in a town. Outline your strategy to bring every person to Christ in the next two years.

    i. In the first two weeks God gives you 25 converts.

    ii. In the 102 weeks remaining, how will you reach the other 2475 people?

Epilogue

Now we can do the same seven things that caused the Jesus-led small group to go out and turn their world right side up.

- Calling people to a relationship
- Letting them witness the miracles
- Giving them a safe place during opposition
- Helping them solve inner conflicts
- Giving them deeper teaching
- Teaching them with a reproducible style
- Sending them out to make disciples

Let's follow the Leader and see what a difference can be made in our world through the devotion and effort of one small group.

Our goal is **not** to be a little Jesus in our small group. Only to be an apprentice and follow Him, incorporating His ways into our ways. To read a book like this one about the endless possibilities of following our Leader, Jesus, as He cared for those entrusted to His care is actually cruel. Cruel to just read about it…to **only** know about it and not have opportunity to practice it. Let's be creative and prove it can be done. Let's see lives transformed through instruments like us who have received the life-changing Good

News and are strategically related to people who want to grow up in God's amazing grace.

So, now is the time to **Follow the Leader** with the best we have to offer Him.

Appenndix A

THE ONE-TO-ANOTHER MANDATES

John	13:34	Love one another as I have loved you.
	17:21	Be one with each other.
Romans	12:5	We belong to one another.
	12:10	Be devoted to one another.
	12:10	Honor one another.
	12:16	Live in harmony with one another.
	12:18	Live at peace with each other.
	14:1	Accept those who are weak.
	15:2	Look after each other's good.
	15:7	Accept one another.
	15:14	Teach each other.
1 Corinthians	1:10	Agree with each other.
	3:9	Work together as partners.
	10:24	Look out for what is best for each other.
	12:25	Have equal concern for one another.
	12:27	Each is a necessary part of the body of Christ.
	14:31	Learn from each other.
	16:20	Greet one another in Christian love.
2 Corinthians	1:4	Comfort others with the comfort God gives you.
	5:18	We reconcile each other to God.
Galatians	5:13	Serve one another.
	6:1	Help bring a fallen brother back.
	6:2	Help each other during troubled times.
Ephesians	4:2	Be patient with each other.
	4:25	Speak truthfully with one another.

	4:25	We're all connected to each other.
	4:32	Be kind to one another.
	4:32	Be compassionate to one another.
	4:32	Forgive one another.
	5:19	Speak to one another with psalms, hymns and spiritual songs.
	5:21	Submit to each other.
Philippians	1:27	Work and struggle side by side.
	2:2	Agree wholeheartedly with each other.
	2:3	Give preference to each other.
	2:4	Look to the interests of one another.
Colossians	2:2	Be knit together in one heart and purpose.
	3:13	Bear with one another.
	3:13	Forgive each other.
	3:16	Teach each other.
	3:16	Counsel each other.
1 Thessalonians	4:9	Love one another.
	4:18	Encourage one another.
	5:11	Encourage one another.
	5:11	Build one another up.
	5:13	Live in peace with one another.
	5:15	Do good to one another.
Hebrews	3:13	Warn each other.
	6:11	Love each other as long as you live.
	10:24	Spur one another to good works.
	10:25	Meet with each other.
	10:25	Encourage one another.
	13:1	Love one another.

James	3:18	Treat each other with dignity.
	5:16	Confess your sins to one another.
	5:16	Pray for one another for healing.
1 Peter	1:22	Love one another.
	2:17	Love your brothers and sisters in Christ.
	3:8	Live in harmony with one another.
	4:9	Offer hospitality to one another.
	4:10	Use your gifts to serve each other.
	5:5	Serve each other.
	5:14	Greet each other in Christian love.
1 John	1:7	Have fellowship with each other.
	3:11	Love one another.
	3:16	Lay down your lives for one another.
	3:18	Love each other in actions.
	3:23	Love one another.
	4:7	Love one another.
	4:11	Love one another.
2 John	5	Love one another.
1 Corinthians	4:6	Don't take pride over against one another.
Galatians	5:15	Don't destroy each other
	5:26	Don't envy one another
	5:26	Don't provoke each other
Colossians	3:9	Don't lie to each other
James	5:9	Don't grumble against one another

Appenndix B

THE BENEFITS OF A SMALL GROUP DICUSSION GUIDE

THE BENEFITS OF A SMALL GROUP DISCUSSION GUIDE which follows **the Scripture** the pastor/teacher used in the large group event.

1. It allows the pastor to communicate directly and effectively with those who are participating in small groups what God has placed in his/her heart.
2. The pastor has the assurance that the Scripture is being applied, not just heard.
3. By using the discussion questions that are answered from open Bibles, it lets the Bible speak for itself instead of hearing what an author says the Bible says.
4. The discussion guide is easily transferable so the apprentice can lead the group when the leader is either present and coaching or absent.
5. There is a continuous emphasis on application and accountability (Matthew 7:24–27) beyond Bible knowledge.
6. The possibilities of unbiblical teaching being promoted is decreased.
7. More apprentice leaders can be raised up because they know they don't have to come up with their own lesson each week.
8. Less preparation time is required for the small group leader, resulting in fewer leaders lost to "burn out."
9. Even though every group will have its unique ways of discussing the Bible passage, there will be unity of thought and direction in the entire church body.
10. There will be less "group hopping" because comparison and competition is discouraged since everyone is using the same discussion guide.

11. Multiplied groups are easier to supervise if they are all going the same direction.
12. Accountability and koinonia are both possible among all the small group leaders in a local church because they are working together with the same discussion topics.
13. New people are able to enter the group at any time since they are not coming in the middle of a curriculum; each discussion guide stands on its own whether a person has heard the pastor's sermon or not.
14. Adult Christian Education classes are able to fulfill their role of teaching content-oriented material such as: basic doctrine, advanced doctrine, topical electives and/or book series.

Appenndix C

PRINCIPLES FOR EFFECTIVE DISCUSSION GUIDES

1. **LIFE CENTERED.** Since our goal is Bible application, the discussion guide we want to use needs to be practical and personal in the way it is put together. To do a series of lessons on the Trinity, for example, would be very helpful for a class to study, but not in a small group. Why? Because our people need to know the doctrinal aspects of the Trinity, but they can't go out and do one. The Word of God is studied in a small group, but it is life-oriented more than an academic exercise. The education ministry of the church provides for that.

2. **GOOD QUESTIONS.** Good discussion guides have good questions. Good questions, first of all, are not the kind that are answered yes or no. Unless there is a follow-up question of a "Why or Why Not?" after the question, there is no discussion. We want high participation in the discussion about the truth of God's Word, and there are basically three kinds of questions that yield high participation.

    a. Non-threatening. There are no wrong answers to these questions. They serve as starters toward the topic to be discussed after the Bibles are opened.

    b. Biblical. We want the Bible to enter into the dialogue and it will if we write questions that can be answered from the text. After we read a verse or two we don't want to ask, "What does this mean to you?" because that yields to the swapping of opinions and the open Bible is not allowed to speak for itself. A better question would be, "What are the two things Jesus said for us to do here? Which of those would be the most difficult for you to put into your life?"

c. Personal. Some questions need to address the experiences the people have had or are experiencing or want to experience.

3. **QUESTIONS ANSWER QUESTIONS.** A good discussion guide will have other questions being asked that are not written down—and those are the best. New questions are asked in groups where freedom reigns. If time pressure is present, people tend to keep their personal questions to themselves. So relax and welcome interruptions from seeking hearts.

4. **DISCUSSION GUIDE PREPARATION.** Many churches are discovering the power of writing their own discussion guides from the same Scripture that is being taught on Sunday. The teacher doesn't want to just be a "dispenser of information," but the forum is designed as a monologue. By having application-oriented questions ready for small groups to use gives the large group teacher the assurance that their people have opportunity to put the truth of Scripture into daily life.

From: Floyd L. Schwanz, *Growing Small Groups,* (Kansas City, MO) Beacon Hill Press, 1995, pages 170–73.

Appenndix D

REDEMPTIVE INTIMACY

My son, Mark, introduced me to a book by Dick Westley, a professor at the Loyola University of Chicago. *Redemptive Intimacy—A New Perspective for the Journey to Adult Faith* is written by a Catholic to Catholics and published by a Catholic organization. I gained so much from the entire book but want to quote two brief paragraphs for your consideration.

> The parish cannot be the basic unit of Church because it is a *secondary community* whose major purpose is to offer programs and services and to gather large numbers in public acts of worship. Intimacy and faith-sharing cannot be the primary objective of a parish simply because there are too many people involved. The parish itself, then, is supposed to be built on *primary communities* where intimacy, interpersonal relations, and faith sharing can occur with regularity. A parish not based upon many different primary communities is a parish in trouble. Its people come together on Sunday, attend services, hear a short homily, and that is the end of it. Religious people and gospel-consumers may think that more than enough, but for people of faith and gospel-creators that is just not enough Christian formation to keep them alive in the Lord. They want, need, and have a right to more.
>
> The importance of these kinds of basic communities cannot be overestimated, because Sunday liturgies are just not enough to keep the faith alive in us when our culture daily bombards us with values that contradict the Gospel and hinder the Coming of the Kingdom. A vital parish is really like a diocese. It is composed of many different base communities, and the pastor is really like a bishop, because he has not only his large congregation to shepherd, but a host of smaller groups which constitute that larger constituency.

Appenndix A

A COMPARISON OF DISCIPLESHIP AND EVANGELISM

This chart assumes an evangelist continues to reach one person every day, and a discipler trains one person each year, who then trains one person each year, et cetera.

Year	Evangelist	Discipler
1	365	2
2	730	4
3	1095	8
4	1460	16
5	1825	32
6	2190	64
7	2555	128
8	2920	256
9	3285	512
10	3650	1024
11	4015	2048
12	4380	4096
13	4745	8192
14	5110	16,384
15	5475	32,768
16	5840	65,536
17	6205	131,072

Year	Evangelist	Discipler
18	6570	262,144
19	6935	524,288
20	7300	1,048,576
21	7665	2,097,152
22	8030	4,194,304
23	8395	8,388,608
24	8760	16,777,216
25	9125	33,554,432
26	9490	67,108,864
27	9855	134,217,728
28	10,220	268,435,456
29	10,585	536,870,912
30	10,950	1,073,741,824
31	11,315	2,147,483,648
32	11,680	4,294,967,296

From: *The Making of a Disciple* by Keith Phillips, Revell, 1981, p. 23.

Notes

Chapter One

1. Michael Wilkins, *Following the Master* (Grand Rapids: Zondervan, 1992), p 132.
2. ibid. p 134.
3. Michael Gerber, *The E-Myth Revisited* (New York: HarperCollins, 1995), p 84.
4. Dallas Willard, *The Divine Conspiracy* (New York: HarperCollins, 1998), p 281.

Chapter Two

1. Robert Coleman, *The Master Plan of Evangelism* (Grand Rapids: Revell, 1963), p 39.
2. Gordon Fee, *Paul, the Spirit, and the People of God* (Peabody, MS: Hendrickson, 1996), pp 63 and 72.

Chapter Three

1. James Stewart, *The Life and Teaching of Jesus Christ* (New York: Abingdon, no date found), pp 90–91.
2. Dick Westley, *Good Things Happen* (Mystic, CT: Twenty-Third, 1992), pp 43, 46.

Chapter Four

1. Robert Bellah, *Habits of the Heart* (Berkeley: University of California, 1985), p 28.
2. Richard Meyer, *One Anothering* (San Diego: LuraMedia, 1990), pp 79–82.
3. Larry Crabb, *The Safest Place on Earth* (Nashville: Word, 1999), p 32.
4. ibid. p 34.

Chapter Five

1. Alexander Bruce, *The Training of the Twelve* (Grand Rapids: Kregel, 1971), p 289.

Chapter Six

1. Reuel Howe, *The Miracle of Dialogue* (New York: Seabury, 1963), p 5.
2. Albert Wollen, *Miracles Happen in Group Bible Study* (Glendale: Regal, 1976), pp 69–70.

3. ibid. p 77.

4. Joel Comiskey, *How to Lead a Great Cell Group Meeting* (Houston: Touch, 2001), pp 63–71.

CHAPTER SEVEN

1. Keith Phillips, *The Making of a Disciple* (Old Tappan, NJ: Revell, 1981), p 149.

2. William Easum, *Growing Spiritual Redwoods* (Nashville: Abingdon, 1997), pp 57–58.

3. Dallas Willard, *The Divine Conspiracy* (New York: HarperCollins, 1998), pp 320–21.

4. Alexander Bruce, *The Training of the Twelve* (Grand Rapids: Kregell, 1971), p 234.

5. Rick Warren, *Personal Bible Study Methods* (Foothill Ranch, CA: The Encouraging Word, 1981), pp 22–23.

6. Robert Coleman, *The Master Plan of Evangelism* (Nashville: Revell, 1963), pp 78–79.

7. Keith Phillips, *The Making of a Disciple* (Old Tappan, NJ: Revell, 1981) p 81.

CHAPTER EIGHT

1. Dick Westley, *Redemptive Intimacy* (Mystic, CT: Twenty-Third, 1981) p 83.

2. Robert Coleman, *The Master Plan of Evangelism* (Nashville: Revell, 1963) pp 108–09.

3. ibid. p 105.

4. ibid. pp 88–89.

5. Dan Lentz, *Creating Healthy Spans of Care* (SmallGroups.com/dynamics, January, 2003).

6. James Rutz, *The Open Church* (Auburn, ME: The Seed Sowers, 1992) p 35.

CONCLUSION

1. James Harnish, *Mark's Endless Gospel* (Wilmore, KY: Bristol Books, 1989) pp 76–77.

AUTHOR CONTACT

Floyd Schwanz was the founder of TEAMwork Ministries in 1994 to Train, Equip, Assist and Mentor local church leaders in the vision and strategy of healthy small groups.

TEAMwork offers a high-touch partnership that reaches beyond printed materials and seminar sessions. We want to be part of your team to champion lay-led small groups where you serve.

www.smallgroupcoach.org
509-860-6198
TEAMwork Ministries
1343 Fairhaven
Wenatchee, WA 98801

TEAMwork MINISTRIES